Limitless

How to Identify Your Fears,
Challenge Your Self-limiting
Beliefs, and Fulfill Your Potential

Meghan Sanstad

ISBN-13: 978-1532910111
ISBN-10:1532910118

Dedication

This book is dedicated to the beautiful women I call my soul sisters: Amanda, Christina, Roni, Jen, Nancy, Carol, Penny, Melinda, Tara Y, Tara B, Sheila, and Sharyl. Because you have all journeyed with me and believed in me while I learned to believe in myself, I want to give back to you in the best way I know how. Please know you all hold a special place in my heart.

Acknowledgments

I would like to thank my husband, Scott, who has helped me think, write, and problem solve during the making of this book and even long before.

I would also like to thank my good friend, Karin, who has closely supported the writing of this book and my future books to come.

Additionally, I would like to acknowledge and thank my good friend Valerie for being an amazing support over the years.

A special thanks goes out to Bruce, for his encouragement and photography skills.

I would also like to give a special thanks to Lou, who helped me create my website.

Last, but not least, I would like to thank the community within Self-Publishing School for helping me make my book a reality.

For more on their services, visit:
https://xe172.isrefer.com/go/SPSAP/
meghansanstad/

Table of Contents

Introduction

I've lived with paralyzing fear all of my life. I've made decisions based on fear that led to undesired outcomes, and I've made decisions of inaction, focused on fears that come from those self-limiting beliefs I'd held onto for so much of my life. Fear can cause us to procrastinate, settle, or make rash decisions with dire consequences.

If you can relate to any of this, pay attention. The truth is, you can live your life to its fullest potential; you can become the best version of yourself—live an extraordinary life—by eliminating your self-limiting beliefs. I'm going to share with you how I did just this—the very same way you can too.

My Story

Growing up, I lived with fearful and anxious thoughts constantly. I struggled with what was considered severe separation anxiety as a young child. In 1996, at the age of five, one of my older brothers, David, passed away in a car accident. This left me surrounded by grief, uncertainty, fear, and loneliness, which became continuous themes for my life while growing up.

My kindergarten through fourth grade years were plagued with the fear of messing up in school, which propelled me to hide under desks and have emotional meltdowns. Being tormented by my peers because of this behavior, I came to know the deep fears of judgment, rejection, and abandonment.

At eighteen years of age, I became a sex addict, trying desperately to gain feelings of self-worth. As a twenty-one-year-old, I became an alcoholic, numbing the depression and anxiety the only way I knew how at the time.

Two years later, after deciding to turn my life around, I discovered a Christ-centered recovery group called Celebrate Recovery. Although I had grown up in a Christian home, this new step of faith began to dramatically change my circumstances. In 2015, I began to discover the power of empowerment thinking, how it applied to my faith, and how these and further practices used comprehensively were the answers to conquering any negativity in my life, including fear. I was determined to follow my dreams in becoming a best-selling author and to share all of my discoveries with others who were ready to change their lives for the better.

My "Ah-hah Moment"

Fast-forward to January 2016. My journey in writing this book began shortly after another's life ended, when I decided that life is too short not to go after my dreams. I had been holding back due to fear, ironically (since I knew what I wanted the content of my first book to be about), but the events of that day changed everything.

It was Thursday, January 14, 2016. My husband and I were on our honeymoon cruise. Early that morning, he became ill (from, let's just say, food poisoning). Having gotten little sleep due to his...unrest, I didn't wake up in time for our shore excursion onto the Jamaican island. Stressed out, tired, but needing to rise, I attempted to make the most of the situation. While Scott went to get something to help ease his digestive suffering, I decided to forgo my morning personal development routine (something I had recently put into practice).

The cruise attendants in the medical center decided to quarantine my husband just to be safe, so we ended up getting complimentary movies to watch in the stateroom for the next twenty-four hours, and I, with mixed feelings, decided to stay in with husband (instead of embarking on what would have been my first visit to Jamaica).

At 5:30 p.m., the captain came on the loudspeakers to make an announcement. He informed us that an unfortunate accident had occurred on a bus ride back from a shore excursion in which twenty people had been involved, and, as a result, at least one person had passed away while all of the others involved were being treated in the medical facility.

In that moment, I was filled with all kinds of feelings: horror, sadness, awe, thankfulness, and revelation. I had a revelation that it could have been me. It could have been us, but here we were. There has only been one other time in my life when I had gotten this feeling; it's not just a feeling but a knowledge somewhere in my inner being that God has other plans for me. That other time had happened in October of 2013, when I violently flipped over my car without so much as a broken bone to show for it. At that time in my life, I was a functioning alcoholic, in denial of any and all addiction in my life. I hadn't acted right away then, but today, I knew I had to.

Just weeks prior to this moment on the cruise ship, I had finally realized what I needed to do next. I had been urged by God to step out in faith. What was it that He had been trying to tell me lately? I had overcome anxiety, self-limiting beliefs, and I had overcome weighing my decisions based on the opinions and expectations of others. Then, one evening, while on the phone with the mother of a good friend of mine (someone whom I consider to be one of my spiritual mentors and family), her words ignited the path for me. I realized it had been stirred in my spirit, said through my own lips, and confirmed by at least three friends of mine: the message I needed to write about was overcoming fear—more specifically, self-limiting beliefs driven by fear.

So, following this awakening moment on the cruise ship, I had no time to waste. Life was too short not to put into practice the gifts I'd been given, share the messages that have been placed in my spirit, and chase the dreams I've always wanted to realize.

The Bottom Line

Fear can be painful, but you can step out of it and live an extraordinary life, a life lived to its fullest potential. I've done just this, and I'll be sharing with you my full journey in the pages to follow.

I promise that if you apply the practices in each chapter to your life, and are willing to improve yourself, you will live a fulfilling life outside of the influence of your fears or the opinions of others. You will have more happiness, better relationships, and true success.

Don't wait to overcome your fears. Join me. Continue reading as I cover the steps you can journey through to become the version of yourself—the you that you were designed to be: limitless.

"The journey of a thousand miles begins with a single step."—Lao Tzu

"Courage is not the absence of fear. It is acting in spite of it."—Mark Twain

*God, grant me the serenity
To accept the things I cannot change;*

Courage to change the things I can;
And wisdom to know the difference.
Living one day at a time;
Enjoying one moment at a time;
Accepting hardships as the pathway to
peace;
Taking, as Jesus did, this sinful world
As it is, not as I would have it;
Trusting that You will make all things
right
If I surrender to Your Will;
So that I may be reasonably happy in
this life
And supremely happy with You
Forever and ever in the next.
Amen.
—Reinhold Neibuhr (1892-1971)

Phase 1: Identify Your Fearful Self-Limiting Beliefs

"Don't be afraid of your fears. They're not there to scare you. They're there to let you know that something is worth it."
—C. JoyBell C.

"No one ever told me that grief felt so like fear."—C.S. Lewis, A Grief Observed

Chapter 1: Self-Limiting Beliefs Drive Fear

"Fear defeats more people than any other one thing in the world."
—*Ralph Waldo Emerson*

"The enemy is fear. We think it is hate; but, it is fear."—*Gandhi*

Our fears and anxiety are the most obvious factor in determining our self-limiting beliefs. It's important that we examine this topic because we need to be able to identify fearful and anxious thinking before we can identify which thoughts are our self-limiting beliefs. It's easier to ask, "What am I afraid of" than it is to ask, "What is holding me back?"

Believe it or not, there is a difference between fear and anxiety. In fact, there is a scientific explanation for fear that's not necessarily accompanied by anxiety. I won't go into the detailed scientific explanation (science has never been my strong suit), but I will give you a basic overview here.

I will also connect the dots between our fears and our self-limiting beliefs. Not only will I cover this, but I will discuss the most common fears. These are the fears that most commonly hold us back in life—the self-limiting fears that keep us from reaching our fullest potential.

Fear

Fear is an actual physiological response to an external danger. Fear is healthy; it has allowed humans to survive over the countless generations of existence here on this earth. For example, if we were to see a very large predatory animal, our human instinct would be to feel threatened. The natural fear response would be an increase in our adrenaline, often causing symptoms that range from our heart racing, our hands sweating, and a sudden urge and ability to run away—and run fast!

Anxiety

Anxiety, on the other hand, is psychologically based. In other words, when a person is anxious, their thought processes are causing their anxiety. This can be as simple as worrying, or obsessively dwelling on a thought or thoughts that cause an individual to react or respond in a number of negative ways—whether consciously or subconsciously. The important thing to remember is that these thoughts are often not based in truth, or, too often, we're giving them too much value.

I'm not discrediting certain situations that can cause anxiety. In fact, I can think of quite a few examples that caused me to go into an anxious state. For example, after I was married, my husband worked full time while I worked part time. Whenever I had to drive home from somewhere, I had anxiety. I would work myself into such an anxious state that I didn't think I could physically drive myself *anywhere*. I would call a friend, pick a place to go, and, suddenly, I could drive! The anxiety I was experiencing in that specific moment was fueled by a deep fear of mine—being alone.

It's the thoughts and messages that we give ourselves that cause the anxiety. It's important to recognize in ourselves what those fears are and why we have them.

Fear *and* Anxiety

If you've been reading up to this point and have asked the question, "What if I have both fear and anxiety," I'm writing to tell you that you're not alone. You may have already identified this, but the common term for experiencing fear and anxiety simultaneously is most commonly called a "panic attack." This can show up differently in different people as well as differently for the same person in different situations. Maybe you've never experienced a panic attack or anxious episode personally, and that's okay too. This book is for anyone and everyone ready to shake off the fears that hold them back, regardless of the severity. For those of you who do experience them, my hope is that you will find some comfort in knowing that you're not alone and that this book can still help you, if you're willing to apply what's written out for you.

Self-Limiting Beliefs

Self-limiting beliefs are the things we tell ourselves about who we are. These negative beliefs lead to negative feelings about ourselves. When we feel negatively about ourselves, it's impossible to develop confidence in who we are and what we're trying to accomplish. It's also impossible to love ourselves. When we don't believe in ourselves or what we're doing, or even love ourselves, it shows in our attitude. It affects everything in our lives. It doesn't just affect our success, but it also affects our relationships. By understanding this, we can come to understand why the saying, "You can't love someone until you love yourself," rings with truth. We may try, but if our attitude isn't working, neither will our relationships.

The reason behind this is because our attitude affects our actions. We may feel that we love someone, but our negative attitude causes us to say or do hurtful things toward that person. So, the question is, how do we fix this negative cycle? The answer lies in our thoughts. If we change our thoughts, we change our beliefs, which changes our feelings, which then leads to changing our attitude, and finally—our actions. Below is a diagram of how this sequence works.

thoughts > beliefs > feelings > attitude > actions

This diagram cannot be complete, however, without a real-world example. I will give you a couple of examples from my own life.

A *thought* that often occurred in my life was, *I can't do this*. This would occur when whatever I was trying to accomplish became difficult. Because I thought this over and over throughout the years, it became a self-limiting *belief* of mine.

Instead of simply thinking it, I started to believe it and *speak* it into existence. This left me *feeling* incapable whenever I wanted to try something new. The feelings became ingrained in my *attitude*. As a result, my actions were to either avoid new things, or give up on something I set out to do very early on.

Another negative *thought* that recurred for me early on in my life was, *I'm not good enough.* This thought, again, became a *belief* of mine. It left me *feeling* like no one could ever love me. This feeling led to an *attitude* of unworthiness. The resulting *actions* were to do everything I could to feel good enough and to make people like me. In my teens and early 20s, this appeared in the form of giving myself away through the act of having sex. My actions were also very people-pleasing-oriented. I based many, if not all of my decisions, on what I thought would please or appease others.

So, why would I have these thoughts and beliefs? Why would any of us choose to believe things that would hold us back? The answer to this question is that many of us believe what we believe and don't think it can be changed. If we hold onto this mindset, we will limit ourselves. We change our minds about menial things every day. Why aren't we changing our mind about what we believe about ourselves? It's because our beliefs about ourselves come from experiences deeply embedded in our pasts. They have formed what we think in our minds, affecting what we believe in our hearts, and become a part of who we are through our feelings. Anytime we decide something with our feelings, we're moving with our spirits. Every time we continually reinforce the same thoughts, beliefs, and feelings, it becomes a part of our actions. Every time we repeat an action, it starts to form a habit. So, what is it inside of us that's causing the self-limiting beliefs that are holding us back? It is our earliest experiences and the fears we develop that cause us to manifest these often undetectable self-limiting beliefs.

A word of comfort:

If you're like me, you may find that you have many, if not all, of the fears I'm about to list. Please, pay no attention to this fact if this is your same realization. The tools I will cover in this book will address the *root* of fears. It won't matter if you have one of these fears, all of these fears, or even ones that aren't listed. You will still be able to start working on those self-limiting beliefs even if you don't have all of the answers.

For now, we'll talk about some common fears. They're deep-rooted fears that can cause worry or anxiety that will hold us back from living to our fullest potential *if* we let them control us. These thought and feelings of anxiety and worry also fuel our self-limiting beliefs.

Fear of Failure

If you have a fear of failure, you may be able to recognize yourself thinking or saying things like:

"What if I don't do it right?"

"I'm just not good at this."

The fear of failure is a common fear shared by those of us that tend to have the characteristic of perfectionism. Perfectionism can be a useful tool, but it can also be a detrimental characteristic. In Chapter 7, I will cover how perfectionism is frequently the enemy. I will also cover the good traits of those of us who tend to be perfectionistic, when used productively.

Other phrases you may notice yourself thinking or saying may sound something like this:

"What if I lose..."

"What if I don't have..."

Fear of loss is directly related to our fear of failure. It's not hard to recognize that success requires risk. If we carry around a fear of loss, we understand that "failing" may mean "loss." If we try to succeed, but fail, we may end up losing something or someone that is important to us. In Chapter 9, I will cover the necessity of risk.

Fear of Success

If you're afraid of success, you may notice yourself thinking or saying phrases that coincide with the following statements:

"What if I'm given even more responsibility?"

"I can't handle being in the spotlight...."

"I can't handle that much pressure...."

This line of thinking **is fearing the responsibility and/or vulnerability** that success can bring you. In truth, this is a reality for successful leaders. In Chapter 9, I will cover the benefits of accepting responsibility as well as the benefits of being vulnerable—or authentic.

You may also find yourself thinking or saying other phrases if you're afraid of success, such as:

"I couldn't make all those changes."

"I can't sacrifice _____."

"I can't change who I am."

"My feelings are who I am."

Fear of change is understandable. It is also directly related to success. The truth is, you cannot make improvements to your life, if you're not willing to make improvements to the way you think and act. This requires change. Change can be difficult because it's uncomfortable. Because making changes can lead to discomfort, it can also be related to the **fear of emotional pain.**

The last set of beliefs you may find yourself expressing through thoughts or words may be along these lines:

"What if _____ happens..."

"What if I don't like who I become?"

"What if it doesn't turn out the way I expect it to?"

These phrases are also related to **fear of the unknown.** Many of us find comfort in trying to plan things. We can try to plan anything and everything. This may be anything ranging from our circumstances to the responses of others. We're afraid of the unknown, so, we mentally start planning how we want it turn out. Granted, there's nothing wrong with visualizing success— more on this in a later chapter. What gets us in trouble is expecting a result and not being able to respond appropriately when it's not the result we wanted. This is deeply rooted in our need for control in order to feel secure. The problem with this type of thinking is that we can never have absolute control over our circumstances. We absolutely have no control over others. Any time we try to control, we're causing unhealthy resentments inside ourselves and others. In the next chapter, I will discuss what we do have control over, and how we can use this positively instead of putting too much value on our expectations.

Fear of Judgment

Those of us who have a fear of being judged may have thoughts along the lines of:

"What will they think of me?"

"What if _____ doesn't like me?"

"What if I embarrass myself?"

"No one understands me or what I'm going through."

"No one could ever love me."

"If they knew the real me, they would never like me."

The fear of judgment comes from a deep need for approval of others. It's also related to **fear of rejection,** or **fear of abandonment.** With fears of judgment or rejection, we may think that no one understands what we're going through; we believe that our baggage, so to speak, is different from that of others'. Because we may believe that our baggage is too much, we feel that no one could ever love us. This fear often follows us around when we're holding onto deep shame and guilt. Being vulnerable with others is scary in itself because we think that if they knew about all the shameful things we've done or been through, we would never be accepted. If we believe this about ourselves, if often shows up in our relationships. We may talk to our friends a lot, but never truly connect in an authentic way. We may also be afraid of becoming emotionally intimate with our loved ones or significant other. This may stem from a very memorable experience of ours when we were hurt by someone we trusted. Whatever the reason, we may justify it and never experience deep and meaningful relationships because of this fear.

We may put too much value on what others think about what we're doing. We may have a **fear of humiliation.** We may never go after what we want because of the fear of making a mistake and embarrassing ourselves.

On the other end of this fear, if we tend to dwell on fears of abandonment or being alone, we may come on too strong to others in our relationships. We may crave constant touch, attention, or conversation.

In Chapter 4, I will discuss the importance of forgiving ourselves and learning to love ourselves regardless of what other people may think or say.

Identifying our fears is the first step. Many psychologists and those who study behavior will attest that all we need is to identify the fear and tackle it head on. The problem with this method is that we never addressed the thoughts, beliefs, and attitudes behind our feelings of fear. This is necessary if we wish to be driven forward, instead of dragging ourselves without any direction.

We must also, then, go deeper than our fears. We must identify the thoughts and self-limiting beliefs we tell ourselves that are driven by our fears if we are to successfully gain the tools to act toward overcoming these beliefs.

Before moving forward, I strongly encourage you to go to your local dollar store and purchase a blank journal or notebook. Better yet, pick one of the empty ones you've never written in. (If you're anything like me, you can relate!) Utilize this tool to note your behaviors and attitudes that you feel have negative consequences. Next, write down all of the thoughts and beliefs you hold onto about yourself or your life, whether positive or negative. By doing this, you can start to analyze who you are today. Realistically, you won't be able to write down all the thoughts and beliefs you have in one sitting, or even in one day. You may not be able to do this right away for your actions either, especially if you're not in the habit of being self-aware. That's okay. Start now, and add to this journal over the course of reading this book. If you don't have enough material by the end of reading this book, continue this process. This process of journaling is the ultimate tool for self-reflection and figuring out which fears and self-limiting beliefs you really possess.

An additional note to ponder: you can choose to do this journal on a computer, but I recommend *writing*. When we go through the physical process of writing, we use more of our thought processes; it helps our brain remember and create what we're trying to accomplish easier than if we sit and type. This process will take time, and it will be more effective to take the time to self-reflect and write it down than if you were to just sit and type.

In this chapter, we identified the differences between fear, anxiety, self-limiting beliefs, and how they relate to each other. We also covered the common fears that are most associated with self-limiting beliefs. If you're having trouble identifying your self-limiting beliefs from your fears, don't worry. I will be sharing some more of my past self-limiting beliefs in further chapters, which may spark something for you. In Chapter 5, I will also discuss a way to dive a little deeper if you're still struggling to identify or work through self-limiting beliefs. For now, let's move forward to the next chapter and discuss how we can begin to challenge our self-limiting beliefs once we've identified them. I will also include what we truly have control over, the role of expectations in our lives, and a basic overview of the healthy way to successfully resolve conflict.

Phase 2: Challenge Your Self-Limiting Beliefs

"What is needed, rather than running away or controlling or suppressing or any other resistance, is understanding fear; that means, watch it, learn about it, come directly into contact with it. We are to learn about fear, not how to escape from it."
—Jiddu Krishnamurti

"Only when we are no longer afraid do we begin to live."—Dorothy Thompson

Chapter 2: Accept the Things You Can Control and Let Go of What You Can't

"We cannot always control everything that happens to us in this life, but we can control how we respond. Many struggles come as problems and pressures that sometimes cause pain. Others come as temptations, trials, and tribulations."
—L. Lionel Kendrick

"You are only afraid if you are not in harmony with yourself. People are afraid because they have never owned up to themselves."—Hermann Hesse

There are only three things you can control in your life. Some of you reading this may be thinking, *only three?* Some of you may be thinking, *Three? Isn't she about to give the same old speech about just the one, ourselves?* The truth is that the latter response is close. The three things I am talking about are what I like to call the three A's. It's important to understand that, even though they're all a part of ourselves, they're distinctly different. They are our **A**cceptance, our **A**ttitude, and our **A**ctions.

Not only am I going to identify these three areas of our lives we can control and how to do this but I'm also going to cover how to let go of unnecessary expectations and give a basic overview of how we can successfully work through conflict resolution—a crucial part of setting boundaries and communicating healthy expectations to others.

I used to believe that I had absolutely no control over my own thoughts, feelings, and even my actions at times. It made it very difficult for me to own my actions, because I truly believed everything was out of my control, even myself. So, what did I do? I tried to control everyone and everything else! And, how did that work out? I'm glad you asked. Horribly! Here I was, believing I was out of control, trying to control the externals in my life... and it was a mess.

One day, I heard a message that I had been hearing for over a year. This time, though, I really heard it. Sometimes, we hear words being spoken, but it takes a certain moment from just the right source to convert head knowledge into heart knowledge. What went from head knowledge straight to my heart that day was the teaching *that I could control my thoughts, feelings, and actions.* In fact, I learned that the only thing in this life I can control are these three things: my attitude about circumstances, my acceptance of circumstances, and my actions in response to circumstances. As I was reading about this teaching, my internal dialogue started to protest:

"Well, wait a minute, my attitude? My attitude is based on my feelings, and I can't control my feelings! They're my feelings. They just...are."

Here's the thing, my friend. Reality is solely based on our personal beliefs. If you believe you're not attractive, then no compliment anyone can give you will make you think otherwise. If you believe you're unworthy, then no person can ever make you feel worthy.

Here's a recap on how this process works: our thoughts control our beliefs, which control our feelings; our feelings control our attitude, and our attitude controls our actions

thoughts > beliefs > feelings > attitude > actions

With this in mind, we don't have to agree with everything people tell us we are.

Acceptance

Think about it. We cannot control our external circumstances—but we *can* control our acceptance of it. Trying to resist acceptance is the same thing as living in denial. Many people don't think they have a problem with denial, typically because they equate denial as an "addict's problem." Let's be honest, though. Let's be real. Acceptance can be necessary for a negative action you're taking that gives you unsatisfactory consequences time and time again. Does this sound like an addiction to you? Many of us assume that if we're not talking about a substance, we can't be talking about addiction. This is simply not true. We are addicted to our habits, both good and bad. Habits are actions we take on a regular basis without even needing to think. Don't understand a drug addict? Maybe they don't understand how you brush your teeth every day. I know this may be an extreme example, but don't underestimate the power of forming habits. You can form good or bad ones; the choice is ultimately yours.

Recap: Acceptance is the opposite of denial. It can be simply accepting the way you are, both good and bad. However, acceptance can be applied in a different way entirely.

Acceptance is important whenever we go through a traumatic event in life. It could be a break-up or even the death of a loved one. We have to accept what is, in order to move forward. It seems like a hard truth, but it a freeing one at that.

Acceptance comes from acknowledging a circumstance with our thoughts. It starts with being honest with ourselves about what we're going through, whether it's something internal (something we're subconsciously or consciously choosing to go through) or external (also known as circumstances).

Our thoughts can even be addictive, both good and bad. When our brains are wired negatively, we hold ourselves back from our fullest potential. We are the determining factor whether our day is good or bad more than our actual circumstances are. It's our ability to accept our circumstances and choose to maintain a positive attitude that determines whether our day is good or bad. To illustrate, I will give two separate incidents from my own life that involved dinging my car.

During the summer of 2015, I was working at a program located on a horse ranch in Shingle Springs, California. It was around 8 a.m., and, during that time in my life, I was *not* a morning person (consequently, because I *thought* I was not a morning person, I *believed* it to be true). Needless to say, I was tired. The driveway I pulled into each morning had a gate. That particular morning, as I was pulling in, someone was driving out. Trying to be courteous, I pulled over to make room for them to pass on the narrow driveway. As I did so, I didn't make sure I had completely passed the gate. I cringed as the side of my silver Camry scraped against the very solid black metal gate. I immediately pulled off the side of the driveway, flung my door open, and hurried over to the other side of the car. Along the rear half of the side of my car were at least three huge black skid marks painted across my beautiful silver car (and I'm not even into cars)! I was devastated, to say the least. Mostly, I was angry. I drove down that driveway faster than necessary, slammed the door shut as I got out, and stomped into my workplace. No one at my work knew what had happened. All they saw was my attitude and actions, which were not at all pleasant. So, what was going on in my head? There were thoughts like, *I can't believe I did that! I'm so stupid! My poor car! I always do something to my car! As I got out of the car, I had thoughts like, Oh, and I left my lunch at home! How could I forget? I'm so stupid. My day is ruined now.* I let one incident send me into a spiral of negative thoughts, catastrophizing, and forming the belief that I was going to have a horrible day. Guess what? I did! I decided I was going to have horrible day, and anything wonderful that could happen would not be enough to turn it around. What a waste!

Now, I'd like to compare this event with a similar event, about six months later. At this point in my life, I had overcome the self-limiting belief that I could never get up early or be a morning person. I had overcome the self-limiting belief that I needed eight or more hours of sleep every night. I had overcome the belief that I was an insomniac. The list goes on and on. The most important self-limiting beliefs I had overcome were that my feelings defined who I was, that I could not control my thoughts, and that I could certainly not help how I acted.

I was driving home from a long yet fulfilling day. It was late on a Saturday night, and I was tired. I was looking forward to falling asleep in my comfortable bed. As I pulled up past my parking spot at my apartment, I was preparing to back into it, like I always did. In my exhaustion, I misjudged where the pole supporting the roof over my parking space was. I backed right into it. In that moment, I was on the phone with my husband. He heard something go wrong, and asked me what happened. Granted, I was a little frustrated. I caught myself starting to do my past infamous negative self-talk, but I put a halt to it. I managed to park successfully and got out to check the damage. There was a dent in the back of my car. In that moment, instead of letting it get to me, I took a deep breath and said, "Oh, well. It is what it is." I had to just accept it. There was no use getting upset about it. I recall my husband saying, "Wait—what?" He expected me to overreact, because that's how I responded to so many things for so long. In that retraining of my mind, I had a small victory. In that moment, I could see the coping skills I had begun to utilize working in my life, and I realized that using my ability of acceptance could get me through any hardship in life, big or small.

Attitude

We do have control of our attitude. We may not be able to control bad events or life-altering traumas that happen to us, but we do have the ability to decide what our attitude will be. We can decide to be bitter and angry or we can decide to be grateful for what we do have and hopeful for the future. Our attitude is a direct reflection of the thoughts we choose to entertain, the beliefs we've left unchallenged, and the feelings we choose to dwell on. Having a good attitude can be as simple as accepting our circumstances and choosing to move forward while being less affected. In this way, we remain effective in our day and continue to move toward our goals. When we take on a negative attitude, it affects us and, whether we're aware of it or not, determines the effectiveness of who we are and what we're trying to accomplish. The stories above about the two different car incidents are perfect examples of choosing our attitude. The same night I chose to accept the damage to my car, I went inside and hashed out the content for this chapter for an hour before going to sleep. It's amazing what we can do when we keep our minds unaffected and remain effective.

Actions

Finally, we do have control over our actions. When we feel out of control of our actions, oftentimes, we haven't taken the time to assess our thoughts, beliefs, and why we're experiencing the feelings we're having. We may need to stop and ask ourselves, "Is this feeling truth?" We need to be able to come back to acceptance, analyze our thoughts and feelings, and change our attitude.

It's important to emphasize here that we do not, ultimately, have control of other people's three As. When someone's actions toward us are unkind, we have the choice to not respond unkindly. We may desperately want our loved one to change their destructive ways, but we cannot control their willingness to accept their problems. We can talk someone else's ear off all day about how they need to change their attitude—and hey, maybe they'll change it for a little while—but, ultimately, they have to change their own thinking and decide to change their attitude for themselves.

Identify Your Expectations

There's a way we can reduce some of these frustrations. We just went over how we only have control over our own acceptance, attitude, and actions. This encompasses our thoughts, beliefs, and feelings as well. In order to let go of the desire to control other people in our lives, we must choose to lower or, in some cases, eliminate our expectations. What are we expecting of our loved ones that, in the end, is causing us to become frustrated by their choices?

I'd like you to take this time to journal. If you haven't acquired one yet, you should do so before reading further. Make sure the work from the end of Chapter 1 is completed. For this entry, the idea is to write a list of names of the people in your life who are closest to you. They're the ones who "push your buttons," so to speak. Next, write down specific circumstances where their actions or failure to act has resulted in your becoming frustrated. Feel free to write down specific social situations in which you become frustrated, angry, or uncomfortable. Note the details of what is happening in those moments. What are you feeling, and what are you thinking? The last step here is to write down *why* you become frustrated, angry, or uncomfortable. What are you *expecting* from others that you're not getting from them? Once you've done this, it's up to you to be honest with yourself and ask, "Are my expectations realistic? Would I be okay if that same expectation was put on me?" By doing this, you can sort through which expectations are realistic and which are not. You may find that many of them are not, and you may need to start telling yourself, as a replacement thought, "This isn't realistic. I'm going to let this expectation go." Maybe you'll find that there are expectations that are not one-hundred percent realistic, but when modified, are very reasonable.

For example, one of my past unrealistic expectations was, "I expect my husband to clean the entire house on Saturdays when I'm at work." I had to sort this in the "Unrealistic" column of my findings because, after being totally honest with myself, I realized it wasn't reasonable to expect him to clean the whole place on his Saturday when he was also busy putting himself through his online school. However, since I did feel the need to have *some* help around the house over the weekend, I asked myself what *was* reasonable. I decided that it was reasonable to make a list of the most necessary parts of the house that needed cleaning over the weekend and *ask* him to split the work with me over the course of two days. This proved to be much more efficient than simply *expecting* him to read my mind, or getting angry when the whole place wasn't clean. In this way, we shared the responsibility, and it was less overwhelming for both of us.

Now, I know some of you reading this may think it's obvious that we can't expect people to read our minds. If we're really being honest with ourselves, a lot of us expect others to do this. What I've found is that very empathetic individuals tend to expect others to meet their needs without having to speak up because they so readily do this for others. They have to step out of this mindset, however, if they're going to be truly at peace in their relationships with other people.

Letting Go of Expectations

Once you've identified all of your expectations as either realistic or not realistic, you're ready to take action with them. First, decide to let go of the unrealistic expectations. This may be difficult at first. You may need to remind yourself of the eliminated expectation when certain situations reoccur. It may be a thought that goes something like this: *This is no longer an expectation of mine. This is my old way of thinking. I'm going to let this one go.* Learn to take a deep breath and move on. One thing you might try is to write your unrealistic expectations on pieces of paper and burn or shred them. Oftentimes, the physical act of "letting go" helps us to let go of something emotionally. Additionally, if you're still having trouble, I suggest a further step, especially when interacting with a friend or loved one. You can express to someone close to you that you have realized an unrealistic expectation you were holding onto, and how that has affected your relationship negatively. Because you wish to nurture this relationship, you're learning how to let it go and move past it. Ask them for patience while you go through this process. Most of the time, our friends and family are very understanding, loving, and supportive when we express a change of heart and a desire to improve our relationship with them.

Conflict Resolution

For realistic expectations, you will want to arrange a meeting with someone to express your needs. I only suggest this if this is someone you have contact with on a regular basis. This will be necessary with family and friends, but it will also be necessary with coworkers, supervisors, or employees. That's right. Simply ask for a few minutes to have a word with them, that there's something important you'd like to discuss with them briefly. When talking to anyone about your feelings or expectations, always use "I" statements. Never start with the word you. This is how someone will immediately become defensive and shut down no matter what you have to say. They may sit through it, but they'll have a difficult time truly listening. The key here is to speak confidently yet calmly. Communicating realistic expectations takes assertiveness, which is simply saying what you mean with "I" statements while remaining calm. Don't confuse assertiveness with aggressiveness, which usually involves finger pointing and raised voices.

Say what you mean and mean what you say, then offer an alternative solution—or ask the other person what can be done. Make sure you stop here to wait and listen. This can be an agonizing part of this process (it's hard to wait and listen if you aren't practiced in being patient), but people truly appreciate being heard and asked their opinion. It's important to listen and hear the solutions, opinions, and feelings of the other person. It may take a collaborative effort to work out the best possible solution for the smoothest communication in the future. This process will take patience and a willingness to understand and see things from the other person's perspective, without becoming defensive during the conversation.

In this chapter, we covered what we do and do not have control over, the role of expectations in our lives, and how to effectively process and communicate our realistic expectations with effective conflict resolution practices. So, what's next? Turn the page as we discuss the second principle of challenging our self-limiting beliefs: how to live in the present moment.

Chapter 3: Live in the Present Moment

"Let today be the day you stop being haunted by the ghost of yesterday. Holding a grudge & harboring anger/resentment is poison to the soul. Get even with people...but not those who have hurt us, forget them, instead get even with those who have helped us."
—Steve Maraboli, Life, the Truth, and Being Free

"If you want to conquer the anxiety of life, live in the moment, live in the breath."
—Amit Ray, Om Chanting and Meditation

All we have is right now. If this moment is all we've got, then why do we waste our time worrying about the future or dwelling on our past regrets? Frankly, the only answer I have is that it's a distraction from whatever we're going through right now, but *now* is all we have! We're not promised a tomorrow. So the question is, how are we going to live in the now differently? How are we going to live in the present and make the most of it?

Choosing to live in the future is simply giving fear, worry, and anxiety control over our lives. Choosing to live in the past is allowing regret, shame, and guilt control our lives. Living in the past often leads to depression. If we had none of these negative attributes, wouldn't we live a joyful life? The answer is, yes. So, let's talk about what it really means to live in the present, fully. Let's talk about how precious it really is, and how you can make it so.

Prayer

Prayer is a powerful tool used by those of us who are spiritual. If you're not, I encourage you to explore this area further. We're all spiritual beings. When we leave this part of us untapped, we're missing something. If it helps, this may be the Higher Power of your choosing. My examples will be referring to God and Jesus interchangeably.

The Bible is my personal fountain of spiritual wisdom. In it, is written the following:

"Do not be anxious about anything, but in every situation, by prayer and petition, with thanksgiving, present your requests to God. And the peace of God, which transcends all understanding, will guard your hearts and your minds in Christ Jesus." (Philippians 4:6-7)

Regardless of whether you believe wisdom from the Bible, I found these practices to be true (even before fully breaking down this Bible verse I'd heard repeatedly)! When we're anxious or worried, we need to come to a spiritual place.

Meditation

Meditation is a wonderful tool that can be learned and used for both the spiritual and nonspiritual. Many people who have never done meditation or have never had a spiritual experience often end up having their own spiritual experience as a result of meditating for the first time.

Personally, the first two times that I did meditation, I had a spiritual experience. In my first experience, I had chosen to go through a guided meditation. This is where someone, whether in person or in a video or audio, walks you through the steps of meditation. In this particular mediation, it was a fifteen-minute session broken up into three parts. The first part was focusing on deep breathing coupled with calming self-talk. The second part involved a gradual tensing of my body from head to toe, as I continued to breathe, and letting out the tension to again relax. The final part of this meditation was a visualization technique. I will cover more on visualization in a later chapter, but to give you an idea, I was imagining my life and myself the way I wanted to be. It was so real, it was tangible, and I felt myself moved to tears.

My second experience was simply a yoga session coupled with moments of meditation. At one point I was simply lying on my back; I was breathing and simply being. I'm not one to slow down, and one of my self-limiting fears was the fear of being alone. This was a profound moment for me. I was simply existing, and it felt so good. I was crying tears I didn't know I had, like a sweet release.

This leads me to discuss types of meditation. There are two main types. The first, and most commonly spoken about, is a quieting meditation. In this form of meditation, we clear our mind of all thoughts. This can be for two main purposes. One is to simply calm the mind from constantly needing to think. This is a rest and relaxation time for our brain. The second purpose is to quiet our mind long enough to receive answers to our prayers. Personally, God doesn't always speak to me in this way. I've been reached by Him through the Bible, through music, or through other people. When He does, however, it's like a still whisper to my spirit. Call it what you will, if you slow down long enough, you'll get answers. He says, *"Be still and know that I am God."* Psalm 46:10

The second type of mediation is called focused meditation. You can use focused meditation for virtually anything. The point is to focus on positive thoughts. You're attracting the energy you want by meditating on it and inviting it into your life. There are many different types of focused meditations, even money meditations! The point is to do your focused meditation on whatever you want more of in life. This is so closely related to affirmations and visualization (which we'll discuss later on) that I'm hesitant to delve too much on the topic. I will, however, give you two of my favorite examples.

It's always my suggestion to meditate on what we're grateful for. It's difficult to think negatively when we're grateful. It is harder to feel fear, worry, anxiety, depression, and anger when we develop an attitude of gratitude. Gratitude, in itself, is a remedy for so many things, even renewing our faith. Don't underestimate the benefits of using your focused meditation for reflecting on your gratitude.

When I first began meditating on what I was grateful for, I found it very difficult to find things to be grateful for. I started by asking myself what things in my life I took for granted that not everyone on this earth has. I started thinking of things like a place to call home, food in the fridge, a car to drive, clothes to wear—you get the picture. Sometimes, even our basic necessities are causes for gratefulness, because not everyone has their necessities met in this world. As I did this, day after day, I started to expand my gratitude list. I started to think of at least one new thing each day. I made it a goal to think of at least three new things every day. At this point, I was keeping a journal. I encourage you to take out your journal and write down your own three things each day that you find yourself grateful for. It may take effort, but it's worth it.

The second thing I started to do my focused mediation on was on my Bible reading. It was a personal goal of mine to be educated in the Bible, and I wanted to memorize useful verses for myself and others. This happens best when I choose to meditate on these verses, so I started doing just that. When I would read my devotionals for the day, I would begin to meditate on the individual verses, asking God to reveal to me what I needed to understand. If you are so inclined, I encourage you to do the same.

Use Your Senses

As I began the outline for this chapter, I sat on the floor of my living room, a large sheet of paper sprawled out on the floor and a pen in hand. Looking over my previous notes of what it really means to live in the present, I looked up at my husband, who was sitting in his chair. "There's something more," I told him, with conviction. I sat there, with one of my favorite snacks in hand, (trying not to drip on my mind map). Ever since I was a little girl, I've always loved Dill Pickles. I chomped down on it, enjoying it thoroughly, while I attempted to pinpoint what I was seemingly forgetting. I looked at him and said, "Being in the moment is understanding that the present is a precious gift. It's enjoying the experiences—with all of your senses." I paused, mulling this over, starting to write down these ideas.

Suddenly, my husband responded with, "It's enjoying your pickle." I burst out laughing at this point (good thing I had completely swallowed my food). I looked at him. He was smiling; I was grinning. He was serious, though. As I thought this over, I said, "You're right. It's about enjoying everything about this moment—even this pickle."

So, what am I getting at, exactly? To enjoy the here and now as a full and satisfying experience, you must choose to use all of your senses. Note the smell and the taste of the food you're eating, or enjoy the sight and voice of your significant other. Feel whatever tool you're using to create, or feel the warm embrace of someone you love. Listen to the kids playing outside, or the wind, rain, or breathing of the person you're so fortunate to have in your life. Look at the project you've completed and admire it, or look into the face of someone you appreciate so that you never forget.

This sounds simple, or maybe even ridiculous, to someone who hasn't slowed down long enough to do this. When we do, however, we're truly present and aware of the present moment. Not only that, but we're much more aware of what a precious gift our lives truly are. It's easier to be grateful about where we're at when we slow down long enough to enjoy our lives.

We have to accept moments as they come. In the previous chapter, we talked about the fact that we don't have control over our day-to-day life circumstances. We do have control over our acceptance, attitude, and actions. This technique of using all of our senses is a good way to accept your current circumstance without shutting off or becoming distant or disconnected. When we disconnect from the world around us, we're isolating ourselves, and isolation isn't a healthy alternative to chaos. It only makes our internal chaos exacerbated.

On the other side of things, if we're finding that we're not able to experience feelings of gratitude or warmth on a continual basis, we may need to reassess what kind of environments we find ourselves in. This may be an indicator that we're consistently present in a toxic environment. This can be within a relationship, our family, our group of friends, our choice of social gatherings, or any number of things. If you're involved in a toxic environment, it may be time to reach out for outside support. This is where you may want to reach out to a trusted friend or counselor to help give you some outside perspective. This will require vulnerable honesty and authenticity on your part if you want honest feedback.

In this chapter, we talked about the importance of living in the present moment and how to successfully do this. In the next chapter, I will cover what I believe to be the most important principle to implement when successfully challenging our self-limiting beliefs.

Chapter 4: Have Love and Faith—The Overcomers of Fear

"Fear is faith that it won't work out."
—Sister Mary Tricky

"There is no fear in love. But perfect love drives out fear, because fear has to do with punishment. The one who fears is not made perfect in love."—1 John 4:18

It has been proven time after time that in order to stop a negative habit, we must replace it with a positive habit. Here's the number one truth about fear: the only things that can replace fear completely is *love* and *faith*. If you love yourself, you know you're worth the journey. You know you have what it takes, because you're valuable. When you have *faith* that everything will work out regardless of the outcome, then there's *nothing* to fear. You may be thinking, *Easier said than done, Meghan.* If this is you, let me assure you, I know! There was a time in my life when I thought I had no control over my feelings or thoughts. Before I could overcome that obstacle with any amount of self-talk, there was something else I needed first. I'm compelled to share with you what it was I needed in order to truly love myself and, ultimately, believe in myself.

In order to reach our fullest potential, we must develop our own spirituality. Spirituality is something that I emphasize in my life and when counseling others, and it's something I will continue to emphasize. Regardless of your religious or faith-based background or beliefs, there's no denying that we are spiritual beings. Our whole is made up of mind, body, and spirit. You cannot be whole and healthy by taking care of one or two of these areas. There must be growth in each of the three areas for us as individuals if we wish to become all that we can be. That being said, I'd like to share with you the deep conviction I hold in my heart, one that I hope you will receive with love whether you have ever stopped to ponder this idea before or not.

God *loves you*. Your creator made every fiber of *you on purpose*. Your body, your mind, your skills, your personality—everything about you—is intentional, and it's formed by an Almighty God who loves you *unconditionally*. No one here on earth can love you better. Even if you've had the very fortunate experience of being loved unconditionally by your parents, they'll let you down someday (if they haven't already). Humanity is broken, and we can only be healed and released from our limitations when we accept that love from God. "For God so loved the world that he gave his one and only Son, that whoever believes in him shall not perish but have eternal life" (John 3:16). That is powerful, friends. When we accept that we're made perfect in the eyes of our Creator, there's a moment of awe. It becomes difficult to dislike ourselves. We realize that it's a birthright for us to become all that we can be.

Marianne Williamson said it well in her book, *A Return to Love:* "Our deepest fear is not that we are inadequate. Our deepest fear is that we are powerful beyond measure. It is our light, not our darkness that most frightens us. We ask ourselves, 'Who am I to be brilliant, gorgeous, talented, fabulous?' Actually, who are you not to be? You are a child of God. Your playing small does not serve the world. There is nothing enlightened about shrinking so that other people won't feel insecure around you. We are all meant to shine, as children do. We were born to make manifest the glory of God that is within us."

This may not be your truth, but this is the truth I have learned that has made all the difference in my life: Jesus isn't just some historical figure. He wasn't just "a good person." He is God in human form; he was tempted, but never sinned. He willingly died on the cross so that we may accept grace, acceptance, and love. By accepting this truth, we accept a free gift: the ticket into eternity with God.

Frankly, friends, I don't care if this is your truth or not. This truth allows me to love myself, reach for a purpose beyond this life, and love others to the best of my ability; I will support you through this process either way. The truth is, you need something spiritual to make it through this journey successfully. We are more than flesh, bone, and brains. If you don't have a Higher Power, I invite you to accept the one I believe is the one and only true higher power: Jesus Christ. If this is something you wish to skip, then the following three paragraphs are not for you. However, if you're ready to move forward in faith, I invite you to whisper the following words to your spirit:

God, I know that I have fallen short in this life. I want to become all that I'm capable of becoming by accepting all the love You can give and live on in eternity with You. I believe Your son, Jesus Christ, died on the cross for my sins, so that I may accept Your forgiveness and grace. I accept this now; Jesus, come into my heart and be the light of my life. Forgive me for the wrong I've done to others. I pray this in Jesus' holy name, Amen.

Congratulations! If you prayed this prayer (or have ever prayed this prayer), you're part of the family. He (Jesus) came to that which was his own (us, His creations), but his own did not receive him. Yet to all who did receive him, to those who believed in his name, he gave the right to become children of God—John 1:11-12. That being said, you have a special place in my heart, and I am so excited for your journey. If this is the first time you have every prayed this prayer, I invite you to contact me by emailing me at limitless@meghansanstad.com. God bless you on beginning this journey with me!

God has a plan for your life! *"I know the plans I have for you," declares the Lord, "plans to prosper you and not to harm you, plans to give you hope and a future"* (Jeremiah 29:11). God has a longing to see your deepest desires fulfilled. He loves you as His child. He created you with specific passions, skills, and personality traits so that you can fulfill your purpose for His glory. Have you ever felt like you wanted to make a difference? This is it; this is the answer!

We must have a profound understanding of our spiritual significance before we can truly believe how much of an important contribution we are designed to be while here on this earth. Now that we've touched on the spiritual aspect, let's look at what it looks like to have faith in ourselves and love who we are.

Affirmations

At this point in the reading, you should have already journaled about what self-limiting beliefs you have been holding onto. These are negative thoughts you have about yourself or your life so frequently that it has become a part of who you are; you believe the lies as truth.

Here were some of mine: *I'm fat. I'm ugly. No one will ever love me. I'm not good enough. I'll forever be alone. I can't. I don't know how. It's too hard. I will never be successful like [fill in the blank]. I will never be rich. We'll never own a house. I'll never get better. I don't have control of my thoughts. My feelings can't change. My best isn't good enough. I can't help it. My husband doesn't try hard enough. My husband must not love me. He must not care.*

Get the picture? Now, it's your turn to write down your self-limiting beliefs if you haven't done so already. This is your last chance, because now, we are going to cover how to challenge them. What do you tell yourself about your body, personality, or personal achievements? Whom do you compare yourself to? What expectations are you placing on yourself or others? What do you find yourself saying about yourself, others, or your circumstances, that other people don't agree with you on? When do you become defensive? Use these thought joggers to write yours down now.

Now that we've identified the negative self-talk, or self-limiting beliefs, we're ready to challenge them. The goal here is to turn them around into positive, empowering affirming thoughts. It doesn't matter if you don't believe them. The first step is to write them. You can only do this yourself, but I will change my negative examples into positive examples so that you get the idea.

I'm fat. I'm ugly.

"I'm a little overweight, but I can start eating better and exercising more. The truth is, I've been created to be perfectly imperfect, and that's beautiful."

No one will ever love me. I'm not good enough. I'll forever be alone.

"I may not have someone to call mine right now, but it's better that I wait for the right man God intends for me. In the past, I've settled for men who treated me less than what I was worth. I need to wait for a man who will value me the way I'm learning to value myself."

I can't. I don't know how. It's too hard.

"I may not be good at this right now, or know exactly what I'm doing, and this may be difficult—but if I'm determined to get something done, there's always a way to learn what I need to learn and practice what I need to practice to get it done. Perfection is the enemy; progress is the goal."

I will never be successful like [fill in the blank]. I will never be rich. We'll never own a house.

"I may not be where I want to be in life right now, but that doesn't mean I won't get there. I need to stay focused and stay positive; that's when opportunities come to me."

I'll never get better. I don't have control of my thoughts. My feelings can't change

"I have control over my acceptance, attitude, and actions. This is empowering."

My best isn't good enough.

"My best is always good enough, because it's my best effort. I have to remember that success comes from failing forward."

My husband doesn't try hard enough. My husband must not love me. He must not care.

"Of course my husband loves me. What expectations am I placing on him that he isn't meeting? Is it reasonable? Do I need to let it go or express it?"

Use your journal to change your negative self-limiting beliefs into positive truths. I encourage you to read these positive affirmations out loud to yourself at least once a day. The best time I've found is in the morning, because it helps frame the rest of my day—but you can do it at any time, even multiple times a day. You may wish to rephrase your long statements into short "I am" statements. Some examples of this are, "I am wise," "I am healthy," or "I am in shape." If you have action statements, it may read like, "I am going on my daily walk today." Whatever insight you have gained from your self-limiting beliefs, you have the ability to turn them into actions or turn them into empowering positive self-talk. Do this every day, and I promise, over time, you will see a difference in your thinking—and in your day-to-day life.

By utilizing the power of affirmations, you rewire your brain into believing truths—truths that set you free from worry, fear, and even depression. This practice teaches you to love yourself and have faith in yourself—allowing you to grow successfully. Anytime we're bogged down by these feelings, we're unable to reach our fullest potential. There is something to the old saying, "The truth will set you free!"

In this chapter, we covered the importance of developing our own spirituality, and the role of love and faith in our lives—including love for ourselves and believing in ourselves. In the next chapter, I'll show how to break the chain of fear when we're feeling stagnant.

Chapter 5: Break the Chains of Fear That Imprison Your Fullest Potential

"Only when we are no longer afraid do we begin to live."—Dorothy Thompson

"I have learned over the years that when one's mind is made up, this diminishes fear; knowing what must be done does away with fear."—Rosa Parks

In this chapter, I will be discussing what our fullest potential really is, the origin of our fears, and how fears are triggered. I will also cover how to identify our negative habits and to change them once we've successfully identified them.

Your Past Does Not Have to Be a Part of Your Present

You are nothing less than extraordinary. You have unlimited potential, and you *can* utilize it. Reaching for our fullest potential takes a willingness to become the best version of ourselves that we can be. In order to start this process, we must break the chains of being a slave to our fear. The opposite of fear is courage. Courage is not something that the select few of us receive. Many great minds have spoken on this truth; Nelson Mandela said it well when he stated, "I learned that courage was not the absence of fear, but the triumph over it. The brave man is not he who does not feel afraid, but he who conquers that fear."

If we are being honest with ourselves, each of us wishes to reach our highest potential. If you were to rate each area of your life, on a scale from 1-10, how would you rate your career, relationships, spirituality, health, environment, and education? Journal this now!

I don't think anyone of us would honestly say, "You know, I really just want my relationships to be at a solid 2." No, we want 10s across the board! Granted, we may feel that every area of our life could never be at a 10, but wouldn't it be nice if they were all at least an 8?

We cannot let our fear control us if we wish to reach our fullest potential. We do it every day, though...don't we? When we base our decisions based on what other people may be thinking, we are afraid of *judgment!* Or, how about this one: when we don't reapply to the job posting because we weren't hired by that one company a year ago, we're afraid of *rejection,* or is it *success?* How about *failure?* Whatever it is, I guarantee that each one of us is guilty of making decisions based on our fears. How many of us never tell the ones we love that we love them? How many of us never even *try* to accomplish what we would like to gain out of this life? How many of us choose quick money over our passions?

I was one of those people. One of my deepest fears was the fear of failure. The emotional pain I experienced from making mistakes paralyzed me. I was a perfectionist, and it was emotionally painful to know I hadn't performed at something perfectly. I had to gain some perspective, though. I'll never be able to do something new I'm trying to learn one-hundred percent correctly. This is what I've learned: there are only two ways we can fail. One way is to have never tried to go after what we want to accomplish, what we know deep down we should be doing, and the other is to give up when what was being sought after becomes difficult. One of the most important truths I could have learned is this: what I want in life doesn't come easy because I have to face my own demons to get there; I have to push through fear, outside negativity, and my own inner negative dialogue that has the tendency to whisper: *who do you think you are?* I've just learned to combat lies with truth. This is what you need to do, in order to reach your fullest potential.

Here's another example of how fear has held us back: How many of us have never even *asked* for a promotion? How many business opportunities, promotions, or romantic relationships have you missed out on because you were too afraid to *ask?* I know that in the past, I've missed out on quite a lot.

These obstacles in my life all changed when I decided I was done giving power to my fears. It started with a thought: *I don't want fear to control my decisions anymore; I want to live my life without holding back.* Next, came a determined willingness. My drive kicked in. What was I good at? What have I always wanted to do, but never dared. The answers became clearer and clearer the less I gave value to my fears and negative inner dialogue. I was determined to find out. First, let's pause and address the following: this process is a journey. It's not instantaneous.

The remainder of this chapter is geared toward explaining that this journey takes time. If you're anything like me, you could read this book in a matter of a few hours, tops. One afternoon on a rainy day, and you're done. While I applaud you for your enthusiasm, you won't gain the benefits from this book by simply reading it that way. If this is your first pass, that's fine with me. However, make sure you go back and read the book again. Read it and implement it slowly, at whatever pace you need to. That's what these types of books are for! Read it however many times you need to, but understand: you must implement its contents to gain from it.

I emphasize this, but there may also be some who feel they *are* implementing this book quite well but still feel stuck. This is a normal process. This happens when we try to do work like this on our own. When we work on our own, we may miss something important and unintentionally skip ahead of ourselves. If you're feelings stuck—say you've identified all the self-limiting fears and beliefs you can, but are still not able to get the desired behavioral results you want—this is the time to find a trusted friend or counselor. Personally, I went through a program called Celebrate Recovery that really helped me with this part of the process. So, if you find yourself stuck on some fears, beliefs, or behaviors, I'm covering why this may be occurring for you, how you can fix it, and why you need at least one other person to help you in this process.

Fears Have Origins

Our deepest fears have origins. All of the common, deep, emotional self-limiting fears we have—they're all rooted in an event or events early in our childhood. Before you set this part aside as some psychological mumbo-jumbo, I must insist—it's true! I'll give you my own example so that you can see the correlation.

I can trace all of my fears back to events at ages four and five. I had all of the common fears: my fear of failure, which was supported by my fears of not being good enough. Part of my personality is being a perfectionist, so, to make mistakes caused me emotional pain, which I also feared. I was afraid of success, although I didn't realize this until I was an adult. The supporting or underlying fears I held as a child that relate to my fears of success later on in life were fear of change and fear of the unknown. I was also fearful of judgment. I was worried someone would think badly of me, holding onto the underlying fears of rejection and abandonment.

This is also another area where my fear of emotional pain came into play. Because a large part of my personality was to be a natural people-pleaser, I experienced emotional pain whenever I thought I had disappointed anyone.

Now, what event happened as a child that established these fears? I can think of one major event that had an effect on me. It happened when I was five years old. I had walked downstairs and overheard my older brother, Dave, talking about a trip he and his friend were planning on taking that morning. I could tell by their conversation that they were trying to keep it quiet. I interrupted their conversation and asked them where they were going. My brother gave me the name of a place (I can't remember to this day what he said), and I told him I was going to tell Mom and Dad. He insisted that I not tell them, and because I loved my brother very much and wanted to please him, I didn't.

A day or two later, I was in the kitchen overhearing my parents talk about where my brother and his friend might have gone off to. They were very worried, so I decided to tell them what I knew. When I told them, my mom said, "No, that can't be right." I remember an immediate string of thoughts that came into my mind, ones I carried with me into my adulthood. I thought, *Did I hear him wrong? Did I say it wrong?* Not good enough. *Did he lie to me?* Rejection.

On the third day of my brother being gone, my parents got a phone call. They flew out to a hospital in Oregon while my other brother and I stayed at our good friends' and neighbors' house. I would learn later that my brother had passed, and the events surrounding his death would result in so much emotional chaos.

Change. Uncertainty. Abandonment. These all became fears of mine, deeply embedded beliefs, and as I grew up and became an adult, they showed up in more general fears—failure, success, and judgment. As an adult, I remained a perfectionist and avoided learning new things or taking big risks. I held onto routine, avoided change, and planned my days out. I reacted negatively when my days were disrupted unexpectedly. I soaked in negative voices from my peers and made them my own. Every rejection felt like not only a literal stab in the heart but also piercing to my soul. My hurts turned into resentments, and those resentments turned into destructive habits. This showed up in the form of drinking, sex, and anger. I held onto subconscious feelings of abandonment that I became aware of only when I started to really analyze myself.

I know this is a lot to swallow, and maybe you didn't have anything quite as traumatic happen to you. If you did, I know how painful it can be to delve into the past. This is why someone you can trust is necessary; you want to be able to write this out and talk this through with someone who can help you identify where your self-limiting fears may be coming from.

If this is something you think you need to do, I highly encourage you to start seeking someone or a group to do this with by the end of reading this chapter. Keep in mind, the group I used, Celebrate Recovery, is a Christ-centered program. It may be great for you, or you may be thinking it's out of your comfort zone. If that's the case, I suggest finding a one-on-one counselor whom you feel you connect well with.

Events Trigger Fear

If we can trace our fears back from early events, we can definitely find correlations between events that happen to us that tend to trigger certain thoughts, or fearful self-limiting beliefs. If you're still finding you're acting out in any way that bothers you or others, I highly encourage you to write down the event preceding these behaviors. Maybe you don't act out; maybe you simply find yourself having a bad attitude in regards to certain incidents. Be careful. Any negative thinking can lead to a negative attitude and, ultimately, destructive behaviors. I will go over my own examples of how my fears and self-limiting beliefs affected my behaviors in the following paragraphs. Then, you'll get a chance to journal your own experiences for useful self-reflection.

Anytime I would embark on a new job or a new education or career path, I would become afraid of failure. I was worried that I wasn't good enough because I knew the road ahead was difficult and going to be hard work. This caused me so much fear of potential emotional pain that I would give up before I even got to the point where all the effort was put in.

Anytime I knew I needed to make a change but knew it would cause a change in my income, I became afraid of the unknown outcome. Change was scary to me, and I wasn't sure if I was going to fail or succeed, and either outcome was terrifying. I would become paralyzed.

Anytime I was around people (almost all of the time), I was so afraid of what they thought of me. I had convinced myself that it was all negative. I was afraid the negative perceptions were correct, and I wasn't good enough—that they would reject me. I thought to myself, *what if I'm left with no friends?* This caused me to fear the emotional pain that was associated with not being able to please everyone. There were many times I isolated myself or decided not to go out to a gathering somewhere as a result.

Now that you've identified your fears, you're ready to journal about the events that trigger them. If you haven't written out your fears at this point, do so now. You can write these two things in the same exercise. The format isn't important; just make sure you can read it and reference back to it someday.

Identifying Our Negative Habits

As we've seen, our fears are behind our self-limiting beliefs. When we ask the "what if" questions for too long, we start to answer them in a negative way. We start to expect the worse and, therefore, believe it—but that's not necessarily true. The next step here is to identify your negative habits.

First, here is re-cap of mine from the previous examples.

My fearful self-limiting beliefs were behind my actions of:

- Quitting things too soon or running away from challenges

- Not taking any action even when I knew I needed to

- Making decisions based on fear, decisions I would later regret

- Missing out on great opportunities and experiences I could have otherwise enjoyed

- Missing out on authentic relationships

- Being self-centered and unable to love others and fully enjoy their company

It's your turn. From the events you journaled about, add an additional journal entry for the negative habits that accompany them. To gain from this entry, you must be completely honest with yourself. Once you've done that, you can move on to how we change our negative habits.

Changing Our Negative Habits

So, how do we change our habits?

In order to change our habits or our recurring behaviors, we must replace them. This is similar to our thoughts. For example, we cannot get rid of a thought by decided to stop thinking it. In order to get rid of a negative thought, we must replace it with a positive thought. This is why positive affirmations are so powerful. Using affirmations is the art of transforming our thinking. Similarly, our habits work the same way. If we want to change our negative habits, we must replace them with a positive habit. There's a catch, though. It's very easy to replace a negative habit we wish to get rid of with another negative habit. There is a joke in recovery that when we kick one addiction, we pick another to take its place. It rings with some truth, though. This is where we have to get creative and be mindful about what we're replacing our current habits with. I will give you two examples to compare. The first example will be when we replace one habit with another habit without being mindful. The second example will be when we replace our negative habit with a positive one.

Say I want to quit smoking. Have you been there? I have. Well, I quit. It's agonizing. I avoid the smoking sections in the parking lots, stay away from bars, and focus elsewhere when I see another driver lighting up their cigarette. I get used to circulating the air in my car. I make it to 30 days (yes)! Just one problem. I'm pretty sure I've gained at least 10 pounds. What happened? I wasn't mindful. I replaced smoking with eating more than my body needed.

Alright. Here's a second scenario. I've been down this road before. I need to quit smoking. I'm not going to light another cigarette, and I'm not going to gain weight. I'm determined. So, what do I do? During those first 30 days, I chew a lot of gum. I trade in the health of my teeth for the health of my waistline by munching on crushed ice when I have my food cravings. I eat the same way I always eat, and I exercise some more— because, hey, I can breathe now!

The paragraphs above gave just one example of how to mindfully replace our behaviors when we wish to combat a negative habit. This is true for any behavior—even social ones. If we don't like our reactions to others, we can start to taking deep breaths and choosing to respond. The more we repeat a behavior, the more natural it becomes. Try it!

The information we've discussed in this chapter covered how our past doesn't define our future, what our fullest potential really means, the origin and triggers of our fears, and identifying and changing our negative habits. Up until this point, this information suggests that our negative habits are a result of our past experiences. When we go through a bad experience, we experience an emotional hurt. If we don't deal with this hurt, it will turn into a resentment. When we don't deal with resentments properly, they can turn into destructive behaviors or negative habits.

If you are so inclined to delve deeper into this process, I highly suggest finding a Celebrate Recovery or similar program to walk you through these steps. To give you an overview of what this entails, you must identify the hurts and resentments in your life and go through the process of forgiving yourself and others. This is a matter of loving yourself enough to be compassionate with yourself and let go of grudges that are only hurting you.

In the next part of this book, we'll discuss phase 3, discovering our true selves. In the immediate chapter to follow, I will demonstrate how we can identify our strengths, gain a deeper understanding of our personality, and see how our past experiences can play into our passions and our purpose in a positive way.

Phase 3: Discover the Real You

"The greatest explorer on this earth never takes voyages as long as those of the man who descends to the depth of his heart."—Julien Green

"The value of identity of course is that so often with it comes purpose."
—Richard Grant

Chapter 6: Learn Who You Are

*"All men should strive to learn before
they die
what they are running from, and to, and
why."*
—James Thurber

*"No one remains quite what he was when
he recognizes himself."*—Thomas Mann

This is, by far, my favorite part in this process. This chapter will involve a lot of journaling and self-reflection. Learning who we truly are has to start with us. Who we are is not determined by others. It's determined by our strengths, personality, experiences, passions, and our ultimate purpose or calling in our lives. That's why when we give into our fears, negative thoughts, or the opinions of others, we limit ourselves from living to our fullest potential.

Strengths

Take the time to ask yourself and others closest to you what your strengths may be. Maybe you already know. This is something you'll want to journal about and add to as necessary. Strengths don't ultimately make us who we are or determine what our purpose is in this life, but they're tools we'll most likely need to use along the way.

My first journaling experience about my strengths looked something like this:

Hardworking student; wise; fast learner; great reader, writer, singer, teacher; great with kids, animals, people; creative problem solver; a woman of God; passionate; compassionate; giving; trustworthy; an inspiring leader; intelligent; unique.

It was simply a list of attributes I not only had acknowledged about myself but also had been told by others I possessed. Personally, I had trouble thinking of my strengths. Another way to think of it is, *what are our gifts or skills?* This opened up wider doors for me, and my list grew to include the following:

Perspective, spiritual growth, authenticity, genuine care for people, discernment, speaking.

Still not sure I was on track, I dug a little deeper. There are many strengths tests that can be found online. At the time I took the test I'd found, it cost about $7.00. Personally, I think it was worth the insight. After doing this, I was able to identify my current top strengths, confirming some of the ones I'd identified and even adding some additional insight:

Perspective, spiritual growth, authenticity, gratitude, love of learning.

What's interesting about this list is that I didn't always have these strengths activated. Just from what I've gotten the chance to tell you about my story, I was an active sex addict and an alcoholic. From this experience alone, I can tell you that I was unable to be completely authentic, unable to grow spiritually, unable to have a good sense of perspective, and unable to be grateful in my misery.

The last strength, love of learning, is an interesting one as well. Remember how I said I hated learning new things? My fear of failure often held me back. This changed when I started going through this process I'm walking you through; it all changed.

Take the time now (if you haven't already) to list your strengths. Maybe your strengths are strong values or morals that you've never considered strengths before. Maybe they are skills you don't give yourself enough credit for. Ask those closest to you for their insights. Don't be concerned if you think their insight doesn't match up; oftentimes, you're blind to the good things about yourself before you either learn to love yourself or practice using your strengths.

Personality

It's important to note what your personality is like when considering who you are and, ultimately, what your purpose is in this life. Wherever it is, you're sure to thrive. You need to be able to identify if you're an *extrovert* or an *introvert,* if you prefer *routine* or *variety,* if you're more of a *thinker* or a *feeler,* and if you work better *individually* or as part of a *team.* It's important to grow in areas we're uncomfortable with, but it's also important to know in which circumstances we'll ultimately *thrive.* The best personality examples I found for this assignment was when looking at the four temperaments. They're called choleric, sanguine, phlegmatic, and melancholic. I would encourage you to look up these descriptions on your favorite search engine.

My test result showed that I was a sanguine. As a sanguine, I tend to be an optimistic, extroverted, impulsive, activity-prone, and persuasive person. I'm charismatic and magnetic, because the tendency associated with this temperament type is to be receptive of others and to build relationships quickly. I smile and talk a lot. I also tend to be boisterous. I'm people oriented, and tend to dislike solitude. I also have the sanguine tendency to be sensitive and compassionate. I'm creative and often daydream. I can also change my focus and interest in an instant, because I tend to lose interest in a task when it's no longer fun. Without discipline, it's difficult to control my emotions. I fear rejection and others viewing me as unsuccessful. At the same time, I have a shameless nature when I'm certain what I'm doing is the right thing, and I'm very confident.

When reading this description (this is a summary of two different descriptions of a Sanguine that I found online), I found it matched me well. When I tried to answer the questions about being one way or the other, it was more difficult. Was I an extrovert or an introvert? After all, I like socializing, but I like my alone time too! I like a routine life (or so I thought), but I like variety in my meals! I'm a thinker and a feeler for sure (aren't we all)? Better yet, I may prefer to work alone, but I'm a good team player too! (I'm pretty sure my perfectionism was answering this question, because I'm certain I cannot be everything at all times). By taking into account the accuracy of this test, I began to understand where my tendencies lean toward. Yes, I like my alone time once in a while, but I *thrive* around people. Yes, I like routine, but I get *bored* without variety and spontaneity. In the past few years, I hadn't kept a steady job. It wasn't because I wasn't any good. I just became restless for one reason or another. I constantly want to grow and move forward. This leads to my thinking about working individually or on a team. As a Sanguine, I'm supposed to work well with others—and I thought so too! However, I thrive when I'm working at something I'm passionate about on my own—then I bring it to others. Lastly, sure I think a lot, but a lot of those thoughts have ingrained emotional power behind them—let's face it, I'm an emotional person. On the plus side, it means I'm sensitive and compassionate toward others.

So, what now? I encourage you to search for a test that will identify one of these four temperaments. It also doesn't hurt to look up all four descriptions beforehand to get an idea of which one you might be. It's important to know who you are because you'll never reach your fullest potential by comparing yourself to others or trying to copy someone else. You can't be the world's best copycat. That's not an accomplishment.

Experiences

What are you going to do with your past experiences? If you've had great ones, are you going to share them with others? If you've had bad past experiences (I can totally identify with this one), how are you going to move through it so that one day you can help others? I believe we're all meant to go through our own struggles so that we can overcome and help others who need encouragement to do so as well. If you're at a dark place right now, I encourage you to keep this in perspective.

Everyone goes through stresses in life; everyone has to learn how to balance their life (or not). One of the most noticeable traits of success we can identify in someone else is when they're balancing their life. Our spirituality, personal development, family relationships, work life, and friendships—they're all a part of this. The question is, if we haven't been doing a good job with managing our time in the past, are we going to start today? Our past experiences don't have to define our today or our tomorrow.

This is why it's especially important to let go of any beliefs or expectations we have regarding our life based on our past experiences. This can be difficult. If we listen to our negative voice telling us, "What makes you think you can do that? You've never done that before," we'll never create the life we want for ourselves. If we look at our current relationships and expect to be treated the same way we were treated in our past relationships, we'll never have healthy relationships.

One of the most important things you can do for yourself if you're living in the past (which is called regret) is to forgive where you need to forgive. If you're beating yourself up, forgive yourself. If you're holding a grudge, forgive whomever it is. Forgiveness isn't for the other person. It's for your own inner peace. Forgiveness is not equivalent to trust, either. Forgiveness can be instant, but trust must be earned. Don't confuse the two and think that if you forgive someone, you have to let them back into your life or even confront them with it. Forgiveness can be as simple as speaking it to your own spirit. It's releasing the control that resentment, bitterness, and anger have over your life.

This process for me involved forgiving myself for the things I felt guilty or shameful about and loving myself again. These were things as far back as when I was five years old. You may have some of these too; either way, it's okay. I began forgiving my offenders one by one. I prayed for guidance in this process, taking each moment as it presented itself. It was never forced. Some people I confronted and walked away from, some I wrote a letter to that I burned, and some I confronted and rebuilt relationships with.

This process has also involved becoming a leader in my recovery program, the one that helped me through my addictions and anxiety with loving and supportive people. It has involved inventorying all my experiences and asking myself who I can help one day. One of the results has been writing this book.

This is one of the most empowering processes, especially if you're struggling with your past. I encourage you to journal about your past experiences and think how you might utilize that experience to launch you forward in the future. What group or groups of people could you help?

You may not think you could, but I guarantee you that, regardless of what your story is, someone needs to hear it.

Passions

Think back to when you were a kid. What were you passionate about? What was your pretend play often centered around? What did you love to do? What activities did you prefer doing? What were you great at? What did you get compliments for? What were your interactions like with others? Whom did you connect with? What do you stand for?

Doing this type of journaling for me was interesting. I found several different passions of mine as a kid—most I still like doing today. What's interesting was to see what I considered hobbies today and what I could see myself pursuing in life. As I journaled, I came up with this picture of childhood Meghan:

I loved animals, any and every animal. I grew to love horses. I was confident with horses from the first day I handled one. I loved playing with my dolls. As a young girl, I always knew I wanted to grow up to raise a family. I loved reading and writing. I wrote poetry in junior high and never stopped. English was my strongest class. I was notorious for procrastinating, but I could write a five-page essay the night before it was due and receive an A without the teacher suspecting (at least, I'd like to think that last part is true). I loved singing; I got mixed reviews, but I kept the passion. I may never be a professional singer, but I never let that stop me from enjoying it. I often connected with animals or adults. I had a really hard time connecting with my peers as a child, but, looking back, I can see how it makes sense. I remember adults saying to me as a kid that I was "wise beyond my years."

Your turn! Journal what your passions were. I hope you enjoy the process as much as I did.

Purpose—Consult Your Creator and Reflect on Your Fears

So, you could do this one of two ways. I'll mention the easiest and (in my opinion) least accurate attempt at figuring out your purpose first.

You can look at all of your strengths, experiences, passions, and, taking into account your personality, think of a career you could pursue to meet all of these needs. It seems difficult, but, believe me, it can be done. Maybe pick something that enables you to give back to other people somehow. This would fill your fulfillment tank, so to speak.

However, if you're a believer in Christ, He hasn't just created you. He has also called you to a specific purpose. If this is your avenue, it will take the step above, but it will also take quiet time with your Creator to know your calling. When we quiet our minds and focus on God's heart, he reveals things to us we would have otherwise missed. This is true communion with God. This is what building a relationship with Christ means.

Before writing this book, I sat up in bed one night agonizing over something God was trying to say to my heart. It was so subtle, I thought maybe I had made it up. My husband was wondering what was going on. I wasn't sure if should speak it out loud; after all, it sounded ludicrous! Instead, I looked at him and told him I was convinced—convicted even—that I was supposed to write a book. A book to help people. Maybe multiple books. I just didn't know what it was!

As my journey continued, something about me started to nag at me. I had always been loud. I talked a lot and had to work really hard to listen. God made me a talker. God made me a speaker. *Wait,* I thought to myself, *God made me a speaker!*

I started to speak life into my book, this project. This project didn't start here. It had started almost two years before writing it, when I started in recovery. As I spoke passionately about overcoming self-limiting beliefs and what true success and our true potential really is, I was receiving positive feedback. Words like, *inspiring, goosebumps,* and *wow* were the ones I was hearing in response. I knew I had something. I knew I was supposed to write, speak, and inspire those who needed it. This was my calling, and after learning all I had about myself, nothing made more sense than this.

Here's another thought: if you believe in the spiritual realm, there's one further point to consider. The enemy uses fear to keep us from our God-given destiny. I can think of some specific fears that could have held me back if I'd let them. The fear of public speaking is one of them.

So, I encourage you: journal what you think your purpose might be. You don't have to pray, but if you're willing, you'll gain so much out of that spiritual connection. Think on your fears. There's usually a connection between your purpose and what your fears are.

Chapter 7: Let Go of Perfectionism

"Strive for continuous improvement, instead of perfection."—Kim Collins

"The fact of storytelling hints at a fundamental human unease, hints at human imperfection. Where there is perfection there is no story to tell."
—Ben Okri

Maybe you don't have a problem with perfectionism, or maybe you do. If you're anything like me, your high standard of yourself stems from a sense of perfectionism. We're moving forward now to talk about how to effectively use the personality trait of perfectionism for those of us who share this experience.

I wrote this chapter because we often may have our path all set in front of us, but perfectionism prevents us from moving forward effectively. I know this was the case for me at times. Let's look at what it looks like to move forward without the hindrance of perfectionism. We're also going to take an honest look at perfectionism by looking at the pros and cons. Additionally, I'll move on to focus on the positive perfectionistic traits we can use to drive us forward successfully, as well as address the fear of failure, the role of constructive criticism, and how to build up our own self-esteem.

Common Characteristics of a Perfectionist

Chances are if you struggle with any type of anxiety along with your self-limiting beliefs, you probably are a perfectionist. These are traits such as:

1. Being highly self-aware of hypercritical mistakes—including a sharp eye for details, usually self-oriented details

2. We tend to be the best at everything you do. This can appear in things we aren't that interested in. We may be drawn to things that are a challenge at first, because we want to be the best at it.

3. We spend a lot of time trying to perfect something. We tend to sacrifice our well-being, like getting a good night's sleep or

eating right, to make sure what we're working on is perfect

4. We have absolute ideals, high standards. We tend to be "black or white," going from one extreme to the other; there's no grey area for us.

5. We tend to be the harshest critic of ourselves. We don't need anyone else to tell us that we're wrong, because we're already beating ourselves up. As a perfectionist, there is a tendency to become angry with someone who is giving constructive criticism because we're very highly aware of those.

6. We may mull over outcomes if they didn't turn out the way we envisioned. This may also appear a lot before things have even happened. So, we tend to be worriers, we tend to think ahead of schedule. If we haven't trained ourselves to think positively, we can psych ourselves out of doing something, because we've already imagined the worst outcomes. Those of us with high levels of anxiety may even envision unrealistic outcomes. We convince ourselves of irrational events

occurring and scare ourselves from ever attempting everyday tasks.

7. We tend to be defensive toward criticism, and we tend to have a fear of failure. If we are failing at something, then it suggests we are imperfect. Although logically we may know that imperfections are human, it's a very hard concept to swallow as a perfectionist. There are strong negative emotions associated with not doing everything just right.

8. We only have the end goal in mind. If we don't achieve the goal, we're really hard on ourselves, regardless of what happens in the process.

    For example, I remember a recent time in my life before I started writing and really knowing what I wanted to do. I looked at my life, and I said to myself (and to my husband), "You know, I have a great life with great relationships now. I'm married—like I've always wanted to be. I'm secure in myself (for the most part—I still am going to have my own issues that I work through), my husband and I are self-sufficient, I've found things I love to do..."

Basically, I would find all these areas of my life that I was happy with. I had accomplished so many things I had envisioned having as a twenty-four-year-old, except that I wasn't in any career. That's what I've always wanted. I would then say, "But, you know, I always thought I'd have a career before I was married." I started beating myself up, saying, "Well I didn't reach the goal I had in mind!" By doing that, I was discrediting everything else.

This is an example of trait 8 when we beat ourselves up for not reaching the goal we had in mind and, at the same time, don't give ourselves enough credit for all the growth we had and the achievements we've made along the way.

9. We have an "all or nothing" approach. If a situation isn't going our way, we give up. Or, if someone isn't doing something the way we want them to do it, or the way we would do it, we would just rather do it ourselves.

A really good example from my own life was when I was first writing this book. I told myself, "I'm going to devote an hour a day to writing this book." But I would have only 30-45 minutes carved out because my planning was off. So, I would say to myself, "Well, I don't have an hour, so I'm not going to work on it; I'll work on it tonight." Then, I would end up being too tired at night! So, I had to get over my perfectionism in that aspect and say to myself, "Look, I'm going to write every single day, and it doesn't matter how much time I have set aside—I'm just going to work on it." That worked a lot better for me in the end.

10. We're very conscious of any situation that might give people the perception that we're not successful. To have the appearance of success is very important to us. I think in this aspect, it can be hard for us to be authentic about where we are in life. We may not want to admit we're struggling financially, relationally, or emotionally.

Upsides and Downsides (Pros and Cons)

We've now covered the traits of being a perfectionist. A lot of those sounded very negative, so I'd like to cover both the upsides and downsides to perfectionism so that we can focus on how to work well as opposed to letting those traits become or continue to be destructive.

Upsides:

1. We have higher personal standards.

   This may look different for you than it does for me. When I talk about having high personal standards, I'm not just talking about the workplace, I'm talking about in our everyday lives. For me, I regard my integrity as very important. So, I tend to be very authentic, honest, very much of an open book. I continually seek what it means to be completely authentic and have integrity. You know, high personal standards are something that people really admire in others. Whatever your high personal standards are, when people see you live them, it's a very positive experience.

2. We tend to be hyper-organized and pay attention to details.

I would like to touch on the fact that everyone's version of organization looks different. For me personally, I have to have everything in its own place. When I have a desk of papers, they're all sorted into specific piles, and I would put them in baskets. Someone else's organization may simply be a pile of "to-do" vs. "completed." However we tend to organize, it's noticeable in the quality of our work and our punctuality in our deadlines.

I never thought I paid any attention to details. When I really stopped to think about it, though, it made sense. Don't come up to me with a new hairstyle and expect me to notice! However, give me a paper to edit, and I can have it done in no time. So, I can definitely attest to this as far as work or task-oriented details go; perfectionists tend to be detail-oriented in some aspect or another.

3. Less fixes are necessary later on. As we're going about our projects or our work, we tend to not have to do more work later on.

For example, as someone with many perfectionistic traits, I tend to clean up as I go. So, I tend to have a less messy bathroom and kitchen. Since my husband is the main cook, however, I can't guarantee this is always the case—we have two very different personalities!

4. We can utilize constructive criticism as a tool to implement self-improvement successfully. Once we have learned to love ourselves and feel confident in who we are, constructive criticism can become an awesome tool for self-improvement. We can go from resenting and avoiding it to actively seeking it and implementing it in our lives.

5. We can turn our worry into envisioning the positive. The same way we tend to catastrophize, we can choose to imagine our day going well. This is a way to turn our negative imagination into positive visions. I will touch more on this in a chapter to follow.

Downsides:

1. We tend to have a longer development cycle. What this means is that if we're always striving for perfection, it takes us a little bit longer to learn something because we're so focused on getting "it" right the first time. It's a slower process for us to move forward, unless we consciously decided to put aside our perfectionistic ways—which is possible!

2. It's way more work for far less productivity! We spend more time than necessary with some of our work, which slows us down significantly. If we're too focused on the details, we aren't going to get things done in a timely manner. There has to be a balance between paying attention to details and utilizing perspective—seeing the big picture. Having perfectionist traits and really wanting to do a good job is about finding that balance between quality work and getting it done in a timely manner—also known as efficiency!

3. It's not always reasonable. Maybe we really shouldn't spend a lot of time on a

project if there's a time crunch. Depending on the situation, maybe we have clients who pay us by the hour, and they won't want us to do the job anymore when they spend so much paying us on an hourly rate—they may be seeing that we spend a lot of time on a job that can be done in less time.

4. It can drive us to our breaking point and make us sick with worry. The bottom line is, at what point do our perfectionistic traits turn into stress and anxiety? We have to ask ourselves, what is anxiety? It's closely related to fear and expectations— so trying to get everything done absolutely right can cause us to become very stressed and irrational. We tend to imagine the worst—and even the irrational. This is a part of making ourselves sick with worry.

I know I've experienced both of these things. I've also seen people I know struggle with anxiety-related disorders, such as OCD. At what point have we trained ourselves to develop anxiety-fueled behaviors? I know OCD gets thrown around lightly and joked about (I'm sure I've been guilty of this before), but it's a very real struggle. So, what we're talking about is important. Perfectionism can inevitably affect us in a negative way if we don't change our thoughts about how we're going to handle these traits.

Mistakes Are Inevitable—Failure Is a Choice

We have to change our perspective about what failure actually is. Mistakes are not the same as failure. Although, for us perfectionists, it can feel that way. Mistakes are going to happen. We get this fear of failure from the embarrassment of making mistakes, perhaps experiencing loss. As we move toward success, there are going to be times when we fall. We're going to make mistakes. Only by going through this process can we begin to learn how to go about what we need to do the right way. To fear those mistakes just holds us back from true success. We cannot move forward until we embrace this truth.

Mistake are inevitable, but failure is a choice. The only times we truly fail is when we never try at all or when we give up. Part of the reason I sought my journey of who I was and what I wanted to do was partly because I was tired of starting something, being very excited about it in the beginning, and giving up before I truly hit what's called the "learning curve" into success. When we find our calling in life, our purpose in life, nothing can stop us. Sure, there will be obstacles, but when our "why" is compelling enough, those mistakes and obstacles along the way will seem insignificant. They are; they always were.

It's important to believe that what you're doing in life, what you're striving for, is the reason you're here on earth. This is why we talk about mistakes, failure, and perfectionism at this point in the book. This is still hard even when we know where we're going. Too often, when we fear failure, what we're really fearing are the mistake along the way. Remember, the only time we truly fail is when we never try or when we give up. When we switch our mindset about mistakes and failure, we know that we'll never give up because we know success is entirely within our control. It's just a matter of time, and, really, it doesn't matter how long it takes to get to where we're going when we keep that focus. We choose whether we fail or not. Mistakes are inevitable, but failure is a choice.

Use Constructive Criticism as a Tool

If you've been following me so far, you know that it can be really hard for us to hear constructive criticism. Many times, when we hear constructive criticism, we take it as an insult—we don't take it at face value. At face value, constructive critic is typically someone at work, probably higher up; or it's someone who cares about us: a friend or family member. Whoever it may be, it's someone who cares enough to say, "Hey, you're doing great, but I think that you would really benefit if you _____." Maybe they don't use the word *but*. I don't know about you, but I always hated hearing the word *but*. It was as if the person were telling me how great I was doing and then following with, "*but* your actions are really not good enough." At face value, perhaps that's true. What I heard was that I wasn't a good enough as a person.

That's not really what people are saying when they use that word, but those were the *feelings* they evoked in me because somewhere, deep down, I *believed* I could never be good enough. What they were really saying was, "I care enough to tell you what's in your power to change in order to have a better life" or to "have a better work experience," or to "have better relationships." As perfectionistic people, we really need to learn how to take constructive criticism for what it is: a tool we can implement so that we can grow and improve our lives.

Be Your Own Security

If you're having trouble accepting constructive criticism, there's a second part to this process that's essential. We have to develop a sense of security within ourselves. To be insecure is to not love ourselves. Security, or self-esteem, all comes back to self-affirmations (covered in the Faith and Love chapter). We could search and search and search for assurance outside of ourselves: from our friends, family members, or people at work. However, if this is the only way we fill our love tank, so to speak, the moment they have a constructive criticism for us, we may think they don't like or love us. So, we have to love ourselves. There's a reason I repeat this information about self-affirmations. It's really important! The truth is, we decide how we think and feel. Our brain may be wired negatively, but we can rewire it positively. That's what self-affirming words and thoughts are for. We can literally convince ourselves of new truths by telling ourselves out loud our new truth on a daily basis until it becomes ingrained in us.

Using affirmations is just one tool we can use to rewire our brain, and it's a powerful one. Once we learn to love ourselves and become secure in ourselves, we're able to use constructive criticism as a very useful tool; we want to grow. Learning to love ourselves doesn't mean we can't grow. It means we love ourselves where we are, and we love ourselves enough to move forward.

This is game time! I encourage you to pull out your journal that you've been writing in (if you haven't, back up and start). Write down any possible perfectionistic traits you may have. Be honest with yourself. If you can honestly say you don't have any, then you can skip this part. If you're like me and many others I know, don't stop here.

Next, you should make your own list of pros and cons. You can use the same ones I have, and you can even add to your own list. I believe we're all unique and creative as individuals, so I'm sure you could think of more.

Lastly, rate yourself (on a scale of 1-10) on three things. First, rate yourself on how well you handle constructive criticism. Next, rate how well you implement constructive criticism. Lastly, rate yourself on your personal level of security or self-esteem.

This will be an important part of your journey. I encourage you to make your own goals for improvement. When we set personal goals for ourselves, we benefit most by keeping a daily journal and doing a periodic review. By doing this, we can concretely acknowledge ourselves for our improvement and where we may still want to see improvements in our lives. My favorite technique is to fill an entire journal and go back to review it for improvements and lessons I'd like to take away. Some journals are set up for daily entries and last an entire year. If you like structure or need accountability for daily journaling, this may be the type of journal that would work well for you. Sometimes, my journal entries are short and sometimes they are long, so I like to have a traditional blank journal and date it myself. One of my journals goes from April 2015-February 2016. There are no rules, so just find what works best for you.

In this chapter, we covered the upsides and downsides of perfectionism, how to use our perfectionistic tendencies in a positive way, how to appropriately address constructive criticism, and how to be our own security (instead of seeking security from others).

In the next chapter, we'll be covering goal setting. So, if this is a new process for you, don't worry.

Now, turn the page—this is where your new life begins!

Phase 4: Be Your Authentic Self

"To be yourself in a world that is constantly trying to make you something else is the greatest accomplishment."
—Ralph Waldo Emerson

"Be who you are and say what you feel, because those who mind don't matter, and those who matter don't mind."
—Bernard M. Baruch

Chapter 8: Choose to Be Confident in Your Journey

"You wouldn't worry so much about what others think of you if you realized how seldom they do."—Eleanor Roosevelt

"Low self-confidence isn't a life sentence. Self-confidence can be learned, practiced, and mastered—just like any other skill. Once you master it, everything in your life will change for the better."
—Barrie Davenport

Set Goals

So, you have your purpose, or calling, identified. Now what? Your next step is to set your goals. In this chapter, we'll also be covering the next steps following goal setting: how to have laser focus by visualizing your success, talking to others about your goals, and learning how to keep positivity in and negativity out.

So, what makes goal setting successful? There's actually a specific way to properly write achievable goals. Many people don't think about this or are even aware of it. So, let's talk about it.

Goals should be:

- Meaningful and personal to us

- Specific

- Measurable

- Challenging

- Realistic/Attainable—nothing too overwhelming

- Dated—the date you wish to achieve it

- Written and documented—today's date for later review

- Short term and long term

- Comprehensive

- Broken down into action steps

Our goals should be meaningful and personal to us. This is why we want to figure out where we're going in life. After doing this, we set goals to see how we're going to get there. They should also be specific, making sure they're measurable, dated, and have specific action steps to follow. To write, "My goal is to be fit" isn't specific enough. How do you measure your fitness? I'm sure everyone measures this differently. So, let's make sure we've really put some thought into what our goals look like and how we would measure them.

We want to make sure our goals are challenging enough to stretch us to grow, but we also want to make sure our goals are realistic enough so that we can reach them without feeling overwhelmed. Our goals should be dated to the date we wish to achieve them. This helps us keep our goals realistic. We may want to reach a fitness goal in one month, but when we look at the measurement of what we want to achieve, we will probably find that a more realistic date for reaching our goal may be anywhere from six to twelve months.

Let's make sure our goals are written and documented with the date we wrote them. This is for a few different reasons. First, we want to be able to have them visible some place so we can view them periodically. Second, when we write things down, we're more likely to remember what we wrote. We want to make sure we're remembering what we're trying to achieve so that we can choose the right action steps in our day-to-day living. Third, we want to be able to review them when the date comes or when we've achieved this goal. This is a good way to see how well we planned for our target goal date, and it's a way to reflect on what we did or didn't do that helped us toward our goal or moved us away from it. Don't be afraid of not making the mark; this is the only way we can take an honest look at ourselves and decide what to do moving forward.

We should have some short-term goals and long-term goals. This helps us take some easier action steps. When we make our long-term goals, it allows us to have an idea of where we would like to be without constantly looking into the future and worrying. We're setting the long-term goal that can be broken down into daily actions.

Goals should cover every major area of our lives. At the very least, they should cover relationships, work, finances, and our own personal development. When making personal goals, let's make sure we cover mind, body, and spirit.

If you're having a difficult time figuring out what areas you should include—maybe you want to cover more—there's a way you can figure out what areas you should cover. Start by making a list of your values and priorities in life. If you need an example, go ahead and take a look at mine.

My values, in order of priority, are as follows:

1. God

2. Marriage

3. Family

4. Work/Finances

5. Friends

6. Service

Now, you may wonder where I come into this equation. Personally, when I put God first on that list, I know it means a multitude of things for me. It means making prayer, meditation, and Bible reading a priority for the start of my day. It means growing myself spiritually, mentally, and physically. In including all of these things, I have a personal mental goal to read and implement at least twelve personal development books for this year (2016). I also have a short-term and long-term fitness goal. A good example of this is to attain a BMI below 30 by the end of the year.

The most important part of goal setting is to make your action steps. Action steps are the baby-steps we use to get there. We have to take those small steps toward getting to where we want to go, or we'll never get there!

To break down one of my person examples from above, if I want to read twelve books a year, I would read, on average, one book a month. Simple, right? The action steps I use to get there is to read at least ten pages a day. That may not seem like much, but I'll be honest—I'm on book three, and I'm only into my second month of reading! That's what can happen when we identify, and commit to, our action steps.

Personally, I have very few goals. This is because I want to be able to focus on a few choice things in life at a time. As someone who tends to become overwhelmed with a lot on my plate, I've had to say no to a lot of people and to previous commitments in order to do this. I want to make sure my goals are narrowed down in a way that I can take daily steps toward each of them without worrying about the amount of time I have to get those steps done.

One way I do this is by combining some of the areas of my life. For example, when I say "service" is important to me, what I'm really saying is, "I see value in helping others." What I make sure I do, then, is include that in the work I do. Even before finding my calling of becoming an author and speaker, I always knew I wanted a job that helped others.

The second way I make sure my focus and my time is used wisely, is I invite my friends to be a part of what I'm doing! This is a very simple way to identify the positive associations in your life. As Jim Rohn wisely states, "you are the average of the five people you spend the most time with."

Laser Focus

Once we know what our goals are, laser focus involves looking outside what we've set out to achieve and asking ourselves, "Is this necessary?" This is why it's important to make our goals comprehensive. If we can honestly answer "yes" to anything, then it should be included somewhere in our goals and action steps. Laser focus, ultimately, is doing only what you've sought out to do. It involves making sacrifices.

For myself, personally, I sacrificed a lot of the time I was spending on social media and TV. I have my own personal action step to spend some time for me. If this so happens to include some leisure time with technology, I allot myself a specific amount of time. Otherwise, I could spend all day on the computer and get nothing done of what I wanted to accomplish!

There are many tools we can use to make sure we attain and sustain laser focus on our goals. One way is by doing what we just covered: making comprehensive goals, setting daily action steps, and committing to them.

We can also use affirmations. Now, I've mentioned affirmations a lot, so I won't go into too much detail here. What I will say is that we can use affirmations to state what we are trying to achieve as if we've already achieved it. This is a really good way to put us in the right mindset to have a positive attitude and follow through with our action steps with ease. When we state what we want to achieve as an affirmation, we're saying it in the present tense, not the future tense. Making our brain see our goals as a reality helps us to subconsciously allow into our lives only what will help us achieve what we're trying to accomplish.

Visualization

Using visualization is especially helpful for our long-term goals. Visualization is similar to affirmations, except we're going to use our imagination to visualize what we want our lives to look like in five years or so, once we've reached our long-term goals.

Now, some people like to make what's called a vision board. This is a great tool. I want to take you a step further than this, though. In order to have effective visualization experiences, we have to use all of our senses. We need to see what our lives look like, as well as imagine what our lives sound like, smell like, feel like, and even taste like. This is the most effective way to make our vision come alive. When our vision is alive, it feels real!

So, imagine what you'll look like, how your environment will look and smell. Imagine what you might like to eat and savor when you've reached those goals. Imagine how you'll feel when you've reached them! Emotions are a powerful tool, so use them in a positive way when you're reading your affirmations and visualizing your future success.

Talk to Others about Your Goals

We want to talk to other people about our goals. This is for a few different reasons. First, we're speaking our future into existence. It's a way for us to make our goals more real. Our subconscious is powerful; everything we tell it consciously has lasting effects, so it's important that we ingrain what we want to accomplish into our lives in a multitude of ways.

Talking to others about our goals is also an act of faith that we're going to reach the goal as we consistently take our action steps to get there. However we look at faith, it's important in this process.

Lastly, by speaking to others about our goals, we're going to find out really fast who's encouraging us and on our team—and who's not. We may find that the people who are not on our team are the people to whom we're closest. This can be very hard experience.

I've had moments when I've experienced family members who were just not 100% on board with what I was doing at the time. I've been blessed enough to have family who, for the most part, at least say, "Well, good luck" and don't completely tear me down. However, not everyone has always been 100% supportive of what I set out to do in life.

So, the reason this is important is because next, we're going to talk about letting other people's opinions belong to them.

Let Other's Opinions Belong to Them

First, I want to be very clear on what I'm not saying here. I'm not telling you not to take good advice. What I'm saying is to use some discernment when people are speaking to you, especially when someone is negative or not supportive of your goals. When we've worked really hard and have done a lot of soul-searching to figure out what we're supposed to do in life, we want to be very careful listening to people who are not on board with what we're doing. So, let their opinions belong to them. What I mean by this, is to not let other people's opinions become our reality. We need to quiet the voice. We may feel compelled to say something along the lines of, "I understand you're not on board with this, and that's really too bad, but I'm confident in what I'm doing. So, if it's not something you can be positive or supportive about, let's just talk about something else for now." This really relates to the power of association. If we have friends who are super negative about what we've decided to do, perhaps we've just found an easy way to prune some unhealthy relationships out of our lives and start associating with people who are positive, goal-setting individuals. Maybe we can find a group of people who are trying to achieve some of the same things as we are, and we can spend more time with them. Whatever we have to do to change our associations, the bottom line is that we have to reject the negative opinions of others that drag us down mentally or emotionally. Let those opinions belong to them! Other people's opinions don't define who we are. The moment we let someone's negative opinion define us, we give someone else all of the power to limit our potential. It's okay if a negative thought pops up, but we have to quiet the negative voices. This is nearly impossible to do when we're surrounding ourselves with them.

Be Positive or Be Quiet

There are negative voices around us, but there's also the inner dialogue we need to learn to quiet. When we start to hear that inner negative dialogue, we can't just tell ourselves to not think about it. We have to replace the thought with something else. For example, when we hear,

"Who are you? Who are you to be brilliant? Who are you to succeed? You've never done that before," we have to be able to stop and think to ourselves—better yet, say to ourselves, "You know, I may have never done this before, but I have tools now to help me get there. I can do this. I am doing this."

Sometimes, we literally have to turn around to those closest to us and say, "Look, be positive or be quiet." Even just being around our family member's negativity is draining. Attitudes are contagious. If we hang around negative attitudes, we'll have a negative attitude. If we have a negative attitude, we will affect the people around us, who will also give off a negative attitude.

Most people haven't learned this truth, which is really related to the idea of the power of association. Maybe there are people in your life who have figured this out. Maybe, similar to my past experience, you've naturally been negative and have lost a number of friends over the years. Some of these friends may not be consciously aware of it, but in general, most people don't like to be around negative people. On the other hand, negative people flock to negative people.

What is true about negativity is also true about positivity. If we hang around people with positive attitudes, we will be more positive. If we become more positive, the people around us will be more positive. When we develop ourselves, we start to feel good about ourselves and what we're doing. This resonates with others. People really like to be around that. Opportunities, many times, are brought to us by other people. When we give off positivity, more doors start to open.

Stop Being a People Pleaser

For those of us who are extremely caring, maybe even codependent, we tend to say "yes" to everyone—so much so, that we do everything for everyone else while we put ourselves last. When we're trying to achieve our goals, and keep our laser focus, this just can't happen. A lot of times, when we're saying yes to everyone else, we're trying to be a people pleaser. This really comes back to caring too much about what other people think. The good news is, as we develop ourselves to become our own security and develop our focus, this issue shows up less and less.

It's your turn to write down your own goals. If it helps, write down your top value or priorities.

This may help you pick comprehensive goals you'd like to achieve.

I encourage you to write down both short-term and long-term goals. Make sure they meet the specific way to write them successfully. I especially want to emphasize to you writing comprehensive goals, so that every area of your life is covered. By doing this, you make sure everything you do in your day-to-day life is purposeful.

Once you've done this, feel free to talk to others about your goals! You may want an accountability partner for certain action steps in a certain goal or area.

I know I've covered a lot of big steps in this chapter. I discussed goal setting, visualization, talking about our goals, and how to stay positive by utilizing the power of association. Don't feel you have to do everything in here right away. I would encourage you to implement what you can but refrain from overwhelming yourself if you don't currently practice any of these exercises. If you want, come back and read this book again! You may want to implement one or two things now, and implement something new after you've read this book again.

In the next chapter, I will be covering the most exciting part: how to embrace change (and make it a positive experience)!

Chapter 9: Embrace Change

"Progress is impossible without change,
and those who cannot change their
minds cannot change anything."
—George Bernard Shaw

You must be the change you wish to see
in the world."—Mahatma Gandhi

Embracing change is key. We can't let our fear of change, our fear of the unknown, or our fear of stepping outside our comfort zone limit us. Change is inevitable, and if we don't work with it, it will work against us. We have to be willing to change in order to grow. In order to succeed, in order to move ahead, we have to be willing to change.

Personal Development Routine

The first key to change is to change ourselves. We can't change our circumstances without first doing this. The most effective way to do this is to implement personal development techniques.

I highly encourage you, if you haven't already, to check out Hal Elrod's book, The Miracle Morning. This book actually changed everything for me in terms of how I saw personal development. I learned that personal development wasn't just picking up a book to read. It's implementing different personal development techniques into a routine. Hal Elrod mentions in his book that it's best to have a routine that we implement first thing in the morning. It gets us going; it gets us in the right mindset, helps us feel good, and helps us develop the right mindset to motivate ourselves to be productive for the rest of our day. So, whatever that may look like for you, do it. I recognize that this may look different for everyone.

I started out doing my miracle morning according to the suggestion in Hal's book. I found that I really wasn't satisfied spending only ten minutes or so on some of the activities, but I wanted to implement them all. So, I stepped back and revised it to fit my life better. Mine looks like me getting up in the morning spending my first waking moments doing my prayer, meditation, and devotional reading—spending my time with God. I spend the next portion of my time doing self-reflection, and usually journaling about the previous day. Personally, I've found that journaling in the evening doesn't work well for me, so I implement it in the morning. I also do my affirmations in the morning. Depending on how the rest of my day is scheduled, I might spend the next hour writing my current book, or I may do that first thing coming home. I also make some form of exercise a priority in my day. I've found that I need variety; I need structure, but I also need the flexibility to change up how I spend my time doing personal development—so I leave myself open to mix up how I spend that time.

The bottom line is that having a personal development routine will ensure that we're embracing change, we're bettering ourselves, and that's a really important part of this process.

Do the Thing!

Just do the thing! I know this sounds very vague, but bear with me. Whatever you've committed to, whatever action steps you're supposed to do toward what you're trying to achieve, just do it.

I used to be the world's worst procrastinator— and maybe you can relate! However, there are a lot of way we can motivate ourselves. One of the biggest ways is to do what we've already done in this book—to know in our heart, in our soul, in our spirit, that we're living our life purposefully; we're doing the things we are born to do. That really helps our motivation.

If you're anything like me, you may tend to overschedule your work, but you may not take enough time to sit down, slow down, relax, and take time for yourself enjoying something that you like to do. The truth is, it's really important for your happiness and helps keep you motivated for the long haul.

I do a couple of things to help with this. I consider my morning time to be for myself, but I also schedule for myself sometime during the day or evening for relaxation or play. I use a timer method for both play and work. Especially because I'm self-employed, this is really important. It takes a lot of discipline and developing self-management skills in order to manage myself well. This is true for anyone who's not naturally good at self-management—and I'm definitely one of these people. I have to work very hard to be good at this. Right now, I'm self-employed. I'm also going back to school. I have to be wise with my time, but I have to make sure I'm not just working myself without any play. As human beings, we can burn out, we can resent ourselves, we can get stressed and then take it out on our loved ones—and I'm sure none of us wants to do that. So, scheduling relaxation or "play" time is important to maintain balance.

The person I get this idea from is Ralph Waldo Emerson, who said, "Do the thing, and you will have the power." Regardless of how we feel, regardless of what our circumstances are, or what we're afraid of, we just need to do the thing! Especially if we're coming from a place where we've worked through most of our fears, but there's just this one thing we have trouble with— we may become apprehensive, or we may have anxiety. Whatever happens to us, a lot of times we just have to go through it and live through it and experience that we can do it. By going through with the actions anyway, we develop our confidence.

I've experienced this a lot with speaking. In grade school, middle school, or high school, you could forget about me standing up to speak. I remember in college, however, I was required to take a public speaking class. I'm an A student; I get B's in my difficult classes. This was one of those classes. Ironically, I'm naturally a sanguine. Naturally, I have a very confident personality. I let my fear of public speaking dim my personality. If I had just gone in with my true self, I would have done a lot better. It's okay that I wasn't perfect; that's not the lesson I'm trying to point out here. Once I decided to go through my own journey of improvement, this changed.

Going through my own recovery program, I went through a lot of change and achievement in my personal development. I was eventually asked to serve in leadership. The day came when I told myself, "You know what, I've have my testimony written out for a while. I'd like to make it a goal to give my testimony this year." After going to my leader, I was scheduled for the following month. I was terrified—absolutely terrified. However, I used the tools that I've been talking about. I told myself it was going to be okay, that there were people who needed to hear my story. Instead of dwelling on my feelings of fear, I went to work editing my testimony so that it was more current and relevant because I had written it months previously. At that point, a lot of change had happened in my life over the last several months. The point I'm trying to make is that I just did what I needed to do. I got in front of that group of people. Although I knew almost every face, I was still scared. I did it anyway, and it turned out to be an amazing experience. I could never replicate it, but just doing it, rid me of my fears.

At that point in my life, I didn't need anyone else to tell me that I was born to write and that I was born to speak. Yet, when I stepped up to do what I was born to do, there were many voices who told me I was right. My confidence grew that day, and so did my opportunities to speak more and to teach. If I hadn't just gone up and done it, I wouldn't be moving forward into my purpose.

My question for you is how many times have you let your fear get in the way of what you're supposed to be doing? I know this was a past reality in my own life. This is something we should each journal about individually. I encourage you to pause and do so now.

Identify Your Mastermind Group(s)

The one thing that we have to remember is that part of changing is changing the people we associate with. The important key here is to identify our mastermind group or groups of people. A mastermind group is a group of people who are trying to achieve the same goal or goals that we are. Whatever we're trying to do, whether it's focusing on personal development, getting serious about a certain line of work that you're trying to do—we have to find opportunities to be in social situations with like-minded people.

Spend time with them. Get to know them and learn from them. Again, Jim Rohn says, "You are the average of the five people you spend the most time with." If we want to do well in finances, we need to spend time with people who are doing well with their finances. If we want to do well in a particular business we've sought out to do, we should spend a lot of time with people doing well in that business. If we want to be more positive, we must spend more time with positive people! Whatever it is, we may not know people who are accomplished in the area we're trying to grow in. That's when we'll need to look around and ask the people nearest us if they're willing to partner with us. Those who are willing become part of our mastermind group; those people are a part of a team and the group can function as accountability partners for each other. Some will go all the way with us and some won't. It's just important that we keep our laser focus. If we can't find the community, we need to make the community to effectively use the power of association.

Importance of Vulnerability and Authenticity

Authenticity is extremely important when we're forming our mastermind groups. If we have a hard time being authentic, then it's a crucial part of embracing change as well—and with authenticity comes vulnerability.

I've heard it said, be careful with whom you're vulnerable. Part of this is true, but there are two things to remember. First, it's very common for us to have certain friends we talk to about certain things, and other friends we talk to about different areas of our lives. It's important that whomever we choose to trust or relate to about whatever we're talking about, we're able to be vulnerable with them. Vulnerability is about being able to be honest about where we are in life even when it's not pretty. The reason I don't agree 100% with the idea that we must be careful with whom we're vulnerable is because once we've decided that we're going to spend time with the people who have a positive outlook on what we're doing, with people who are going after similar things we're working toward, it's really easy to be vulnerable—once we've practiced it. It's much easier, because we've already identified the people we know we can trust to be honest with. If we're trying to improve in our finances, we can't be dishonest with the group of people we're trying to learn from. It's better for us to say something like, "Hey, look. My finances aren't where I want them to be, and

I want to learn from you." We're likely to get a positive and supportive response by doing this. This is one reason it's so important to be authentic and honest about where we are in life.

Maybe you have a high level of integrity, but the types of friends you've had in the past like to gossip, or aren't very honest, or lack integrity in some area. If this is your experience, it may be time for you to step away and spend more time with the people who value the same character traits that are important to you. No one wants to be vulnerable with friends who are gossipers or critical of others. So, it's important to look at the other side of this; it's important for us to be willing to step back and look at the people we allow in our lives whom we may need to spend less time with. In this way, we allow ourselves to successfully be authentic and vulnerable for our own benefit and that of others.

There Is no Success Without Risks

When I say, "There is no success without risks," I'm not saying that we should make decisions that are unwise, uninformed, or impulsive. Obviously, these are unintelligent ways to make decisions. What I am trying to say, however, goes perfectly with a recent video I watched of the famous Steve Harvey. In this video, he talked about when we know what our God-given abilities are, we have to jump. There's no success without jumping. It's not going to be easy or uneventful. When we jump, our arms are flailing through the air; we're hitting obstacles, getting scraped up, and we get some bumps and bruises. That's the truth. However, when we jump for what we know is ours, for what we know we're created or called to do, our parachute eventually has to deploy.

Steve Harvey's metaphor is exactly what I'm talking about. We have to be willing to make changes; we have to be willing to go through some level of risk in order to reach our fullest potential. I've been talking about "success" a lot. What I define as true success is when we reach our fullest potential as an individual. Everybody's success, everyone's fullest potential is different, but we have to be willing to jump for what we know is ours—for what we know we are created for or designed to do. Whatever we're passionate about, whatever we're called to do—we have to be willing to jump.

Taking Responsibility

Throughout this book, even though we've talked about overcoming limiting beliefs, maybe you're still sitting there thinking, "well I can't do this because of _____." Name your reason. It doesn't matter what it is.

It doesn't matter if we think it's because of our past. It doesn't matter if we think the government is to blame. It doesn't matter if we think our parents are to blame. It doesn't matter if we think it's our ex or our peers we should blame. It doesn't matter! The truth is that if our limiting beliefs are still in a blaming mode, we're not taking full responsibility for our lives.

I was stuck for a really long time, because I was so focused on what had gone wrong in my life—beating myself up and blaming other people. It was things like, "Why would God create me to be so overly-sensitive? Nobody likes me. I get bullied. I can't stand up for myself. Nobody stood up for me. Then, I got diagnosed with this thing called 'bipolar disorder,' and now, I'm just not normal. I'm sick, and I'm never going to get better." It wasn't going to end until I decided I was going to end it. I went so far into this world of not taking responsibility for my own life that when I was deep in my sex addiction, for a really long time, I didn't see an issue with it. If anyone wants to know how a man or woman goes from being deeply ashamed of sexual acts their committing that are against their moral standards—frankly, it doesn't matter what it is. I started with having sex before marriage, which for most people is not a big deal. I had sex with my boyfriends, which, again, isn't a big deal in the American culture. Then, I was having sex with strangers. The further I went, the more the outside world started to say, "Wait a minute, what's wrong with you?" What's interesting is that I was ashamed when I went through the socially acceptable parts of my addiction, but when the outside world started to have an opinion about my sexual activities and my drinking, I started to go from ashamed to living in denial. I started to say, "There's nothing wrong with me doing this. I'm not hurting myself. I'm not hurting anyone. I'm just having fun. I know when I've had enough to drink." The justifications are endless.

It's important to ask ourselves, "What might I be in denial about," because denial doesn't just come in a box labeled "addiction." Denial comes when we tell ourselves, "I'm a single mom, and I'll never be financially independent," or, "I'll never be able to afford college without taking out a loan," or, "I'll never pay off my college loans. I might as well buy a house now." What's interesting is that this last example is a phenomenon happening here in American. We accumulate debt, and end up accumulating more before we can properly manage and eliminate what debt we've already accumulated. Aside from the external factors, part of the internal struggle we face individually is denial. How many of us have done this? I know I've been guilty of it, and the only way I've started to get myself out is by stopping and telling myself, "You know what, I'm going to start taking responsibility for getting to where I am today." I'm not claiming that everything that happens to us is our fault. I'm saying that every choice we make has an effect on our lives and the lives of those around us. At what point do we say to ourselves, "What happened in the past doesn't matter. It is what it is. Now, what am I going to do to get to where I want to be." This is where taking responsibility comes in. So, if we haven't eliminated our limited beliefs at this point, this is one important area we need to take a hard look at.

Are you ready?

Chapter 10: What Will Your Story Be?

My aim by this point in the book is that you, as the reader, have seen the value in the tools mentioned in this book—tools you can implement to add value to your life. My hope is that you've had your personal "ah-hah" moment, or you're at least one step closer to having it. I would like you to ask yourself what that moment is, or what that moment was, or what that moment will feel like. If you're not sure what this is, let me explain. There are moments in our lives when we say, "Ah-hah! I get it." They're moments when something clicks, something so significant that it moves us into action toward changing our lives.

The ultimate question is, what's yours, and what are you going to do with it?

In the last chapter here, I'm going to highlight the four main points you should take away from this book. If you take nothing else away, the goal is that you take away these key points.

Live an Extraordinary Life

I once was told by someone very close to me something that really got me thinking. This person had known me for a few years. They had seen glimpses of my destructive past lifestyle, and they had also seen me go through change and growth using the practices that I talk about in this book. This person told me that my battles, all of the struggles I had gone through in my life—mainly the things I had used to define myself for most of my life—showed what an extraordinary life I had. This person was telling me that with my unique experiences and through the process of overcoming much of it, I had a story worth sharing in order to help others. I questioned the idea that my life was interesting, let alone extraordinary. This person responded with, "Well, you live it. So, what's seen as an extraordinary life to others appears to be an ordinary life to you."

If we look at our lives through the right lenses, through the eyes of another person, we all live extraordinary lives. How do we learn to accept this? One step is to take a look at our struggles and either how we've overcome them, or decided how we're going to take the steps to overcome them. A second step is to look at our lives with an attitude of gratitude. Doing this means looking at our lives, what we really have, who we have, what it's made up of, and choosing to be grateful for what we do have.

I believe that we all want to live extraordinary lives, but when will we accept that we live extraordinary lives. It's all about how we look at our lives and what we choose to do with our lives. Remember the quote by Marianne Williamson from her book *A Return to Love:* "Our deepest fear is not that we are inadequate. Our deepest fear is that we are powerful beyond measure. It is our light, not our darkness, that most frightens us. We ask ourselves, 'Who am I to be brilliant, gorgeous, talented, fabulous?' Actually, who are you not to be?" The ability to live an extraordinary life starts when we believe this truth. Everybody has the potential to learn to be content with where they are and choose to become the best version of themselves that they want to be. *That* is an extraordinary life.

Face Your Fears

One thing I've learned through my own journey is that our fear of whatever it is we're procrastinating about or not choosing to take a leap of faith toward is worse than actually doing the things we're afraid of doing. We must act through our fears. We must act out of love for ourselves. We must act with faith activated. When we're afraid, we don't act. When we act out of fear, we won't get good result. It's important to act out of faith instead of fear.

Hal Elrod, author of *The Miracle Morning*, said, "Fear and worry are a misuse of my intelligence and imagination." When we feel afraid, we must identify our fears as either rational or irrational. The irrational fears we must set aside. The rational fears we can make into action steps in order to overcome them. We can act regardless of our fear.

When we face our fears, when we step out to do the right thing, we experience the fear, but we will feel empowered in the end. I've had experiences in doing this with my speaking as well as singing in front of people. I've always had terrible stage fright. Even doing something as simple as karaoke, doing something outside of our comfort zone (like speaking or singing in front of a group of people), allows us to realize we can do what we're afraid of or have anxiety about. When we do something we're afraid of, we end up feeling so empowered that we forget about our fears. This was especially true for me when I was afraid of judgment. I was afraid of making mistakes or not doing well, and, therefore, others would judge me or think badly of me. However, when I acted through my fear, the feelings of empowerment I had were stronger than those fears, and they were gone.

Have a Healthy Perspective of Failure

If you're viewing failure as something to be avoided, then it's important to change your perspective of failure. I used to view failure as the mistake I made along the way as I was trying to learn something new or accomplish something. However, this is not failure. Failure is when we set out to do something we're passionate about and we give up after making mistake or hitting roadblocks. Failure is when we're passionate about something, and we know deep within ourselves that we should be out doing something toward it, but we never do it. That's failure. Failure when we stumble along the way, where we make mistakes, isn't actual failure. We need to view mistakes as learning and growing experiences. When we can view failure and mistakes as two completely different things, it will make a difference in our lives.

Move Toward Your Destiny One Step at a Time

Whenever you set out to do something, it's one step at a time. This may sound very obvious, but there may be times when you know something to be true logically, but when fear creeps in, you may forget.

I have a great example of this from my own life. I struggled with my own fears, anxieties, and insecurities popping up when writing this book. I've been blessed to have a solid support team. My husband is one of those people who have helped me. In fact, the day that I was preparing to write this last chapter, I was talking with him about something. I told him that I just didn't seem to have the time to get everything I wanted to get done each day. Before he could respond, I thought about what I had just said and corrected myself, saying, "No, that's not accurate. I have prioritized my life in a way that I'm not trying to do more than I can do with the hours in my day. However, what's happening is that I'm procrastinating on what I need to do, so it doesn't get done. I recognize two things that I struggle with that I'm trying to work on. One is that I have trouble with self-discipline. The other thing is that I sometimes have trouble being motivated to get things done."

Knowing me well, he knew that I learn best with visuals. So, he grabbed my poster board and a marker and made a diagram for me. He then illustrated a pattern—a cycle I have in my life. At the top of the diagram, he wrote the word *Tasks* and circled it. He then drew a down arrow and wrote and circled the word *Overwhelmed*. By doing this, he was illustrating that I get certain tasks together that I want to do in a day. In some instances, I may even think about how those tasks may affect my future down the road (since everything I prioritize are purposeful for my life). So, I start to get overwhelmed with fears and anxieties. I experience "what if" thinking (sound familiar?) I dwell on the feeling of anxiety and feeling overwhelmed. It's all wrapped into this big cluster of feelings, which leads into procrastination. Then, I'm procrastinating things that I know I shouldn't be procrastinating, and I experience even more anxiety and fears. I think, *Oh, I'm not going to get this done; this is going to affect my life.* You get the picture.

So, he drew an arrow back to the original word Tasks to illustrate a cycle. At this pointed, I said, "You're forgetting something." So, together, we wrote this related information off to the side. There we listed the things I used to cope with this phenomenon: Food (typically sugar), caffeine, and the occasional cigarette. The three things that I tend to consume when I experience anxiety, ironically, all feed back into anxiety, because they're all stimulants. Any time we use a stimulant or depressant to alleviate anxiety or depression, we actually end up feeling worse in the long run. At this point, I prompted us to problem solve. I told him, "Well, I've actually overcome this phenomenon before." I told him about how when I was about to write a chapter of this book, I would start to get overwhelmed. So, I stopped, and I thought to myself, *Okay, I'll start with this outline; I'll start with writing down the subtopics I know I want to cover*. At that point, I might even experience some overwhelming feelings of doing the outline. So, I would ask myself, What's the first subtopic I want to have in my outline. I literally did what I needed to do one step at a time. So, off to the side, he wrote, "What's one step?" Interestingly, I already had the solution to my problem, I just wasn't allowing it to be a part of my awareness in that moment. I explained to him that when I used this method, I got three chapters done—the most I had ever written during a single sitting while writing this book.

The idea of taking things one step at a time should be emphasized because there may be times when you look at your life and what you want to accomplish and it may feel overwhelming. That's why it's important to not only make long-term goals, but also make short term goals. From there, you'll want to ask yourself, what do I need to do today? Sometimes, if we feel like we have a long and overwhelming list of things we need to do in a day, we need to ask ourselves, "Okay, what's one step I can do right now?" This is part of living in the moment. When we live in the moment, we cannot worry about the future, and we cannot dwell on the past. It's simple focusing on the current moment.

What's Next?

We covered the idea that we all live extraordinary lives. It's how we view our lives and what we choose to do with it that determines whether we get to live an extraordinary life. It's choosing to be grateful for what we have. We have to decided what we will make of our lives, what our story will be. If we don't do that, we're living our lives with no purpose. I believe everyone desires to live a life a purpose and significance. At the very least, I think that if you didn't desire a life of purpose and significance, you wouldn't be reading this book right now.

We talked about facing our fears, acting through them, and the feelings of empowerment we gain when we do this. We talked about changing our perspective of failure, understanding that mistakes are actually learning and growing experiences. We talked about the importance of taking one step at a time toward our destiny, toward the life we want—and how that's a big part of living in the moment. We covered the tools that I personally accumulated and used through my journey to move past fear and toward living an extraordinary life, a life filled with purpose, something we all have—and it's unique for each of us.

There's no universal "right next step." The question is, "What's your next step?" In the end, we're all on our own journey—not by ourselves—but, in the end, we're all traveling on our own unique journey to become the best version of ourselves and live an extraordinary life. We all need to learn how to be content with our lives and let go of other people's opinions and expectations while we're figuring out where we're going, who we want to help in this life, and how we want to help them. I believe this journey, this process, is the ultimate answer to our own happiness and the happiness of the lives we touch. There's no right or wrong choice, just the best choice you can make with the information you have. So, the question is, what's your next step?

Urgent Plea!

Thank you for buying my book! I really appreciate all of your feedback and would love hearing what you have to say.

I need your input to make the next version better.

Please leave me a helpful REVIEW on Amazon.

Thanks so much!!

~ Meghan

About the Author

Meghan Sanstad currently lives with her husband in Central California, where she is a dedicated leader at her local Celebrate Recovery®, a biblically based program that helps those who are struggling with hurts, hang-ups, and habits by showing them the loving power of Jesus Christ through the recovery process. She has two Associates degrees, one in

Interdisciplinary Studies: Arts & Humanities, the other in Language Studies with more than two years of study in American Sign Language completed. With her own background in mentoring and recovery, she speaks on topics surrounding recovery.

If you are interested in finding out more about Meghan Sanstad, please visit

www.meghansanstad.com.